# A Study of Kamala Markandaya's Women

# A STUDY OF
# KAMALA
# MARKANDAYA'S
# WOMEN

Sudhir Kumar Arora

**ATLANTIC**®
PUBLISHERS & DISTRIBUTORS

Published by

## ATLANTIC®

PUBLISHERS & DISTRIBUTORS

B-2, Vishal Enclave, Opp. Rajouri Garden,
New Delhi-110027
Phones : 25413460, 25429987, 25466842

Sales Office
7/22, Ansari Road, Darya Ganj,
New Delhi-110002
Phones : 23273880, 23275880, 23280451
Fax : 91-11-23285873
web : www.atlanticbooks.com
e-mail : info@atlanticbooks.com

ISBN 81-269-0648-0

Printed in India
at Nice Printing Press, Delhi

# Preface

Woman, the finest and fairest creation of God, turns man into the best of the human beings by providing an outlet so that his lust and ego may come out. It is she who with her feminine panacea wards off all the germs from his heart, instills in him an inspiring flow of love, kindness and affection and, then, makes his being a healthy one. Brahma's saying, 'no one knows the character of a woman' is misinterpreted as even Brahma finds Himself unable to understand her true nature and character. Surely, Brahma never thought that His saying would be analyzed as such by the male-oriented society.

There is a considerable ambiguity about the nature and status of woman in Indian society. Some sacred texts give them an exalted status by saying 'where women are worshipped, gods reside there.' But there is another profile of woman. She is regarded as the root of all evils. These two images are contradictory; the tilt in the accepted stereotypes is towards the negative and derogatory picture. This male dominated society never tries to go into the depth to search out the pearl of virtues but, to fulfil its own selfish motive, is satisfied in picking the straws of vices that float on the surface.

Indeed, a woman is a symbolical poem that requires a careful reading with high concentration to make out the real meaning that is hidden in the layers. To understand her complex and rich personality is as enigmatic and difficult as to portray the climatic factors (like the wind) that change with the changes adapting themselves and taking different names according to their nature, speed and velocity. Like these climatic factors, she receives different names, viz. mother, sister, beloved, wife, etc., adapts herself to the changing circumstances and performs the allotted duties efficiently, enthusiastically and above all emotionally. She cannot be caged in one particular image, as she possesses images in infinite variety. While judging her, one should keep in mind that the images of a woman may be different and various but they will be of the same woman. These variations may be different facets of her being.

Many Indian English women novelists have analyzed the socio-cultural modes and values that have given Indian women their image and role towards themselves and the society. In post-independence era, it is Kamala Markandaya who has taken the initiative of holding the flag for women protagonists and, to some extent, winning the battle in their transformation from 'possession' to 'person.' I have been much interested in Kamala Markandaya ever since I read her *Nectar in a Sieve* and realized that the weight and substance of her works have not been properly studied and her contribution to the fictional literature is not suitably evaluated in India. Though her name is popular in America and England, in India, she has not got the place that she deserves. My deep interest and irresistible curiosity prompted me to undertake this study in interaction. My purpose of this study is to explore the unexplored aspects of her women, to present the change in the identity from 'possession' to 'person,' to highlight the new image through a grand tour in the world of her novels and finally, to show her feminist moral concern through an in-depth investigation into sexual and familial relationship.

Kamala Markandaya is indeed an outstanding novelist on the contemporary Commonwealth literary scene and ranks with Mulk Raj Anand, R.K. Narayan and Raja Rao. She shot into an enviable prominence soon after the publication of her first novel *Nectar in a Sieve* in 1954. She has to-date ten novels to her credit: *Nectar in a Sieve* (1954)–a study of Rukmani's courage in struggling against the adverse circumstances of life; *Some Inner Fury* (1955)–a love story of Mira's sacrifice with the background of the Quit India Movement; *A Silence of Desire* (1960)–a domestic tale of the relation of husband and wife; *Possession* (1963)–an anti-patriarchal stance of Caroline; *A Handful of Rice* (1966)–a novel of Nalini's victory in reforming her husband; *The Coffer Dams* (1969)–a tale of an amiable woman Helen who favours bridge, not dams; *The Nowhere Man* (1972)–a true presentation of the racialism; *Two Virgins* (1973)–a treasure house of basic human experiences of Saroja and Lalitha; *The Golden Honeycomb* (1977)–a protest shown by Manjula, Mohini and Usha against the British rule and *Pleasure City* (1982)–a dream world of Kamala Markandaya in which there are no barriers of caste, colour and creed and in which human values are supreme.

Through her female protagonists, Kamala Markandaya reveals the virtues and potentialities of woman by providing that a woman is not inferior to man in any way. She stresses the need to believe in the moral superiority of woman in upholding the sanctity of the family. She has presented 'New Woman'–a wonderful improved race of traditional woman. Her women protagonists have given a ray of hope and a goal to the countless women who are groping in the dark and living in isolation and frustration. She has opened a new vista for women by infusing a crusading spirit into them for the welfare of humanity and the alleviation of human suffering.

It is hoped that the present book will prove a remarkable contribution to the study of Kamala Markandaya's works. I have been fortunate to receive cooperation and encouragement from a large number of persons while writing this book. I am deeply indebted to Dr. Sushma Sharma, Dean of Art Faculty, M.J.P. Rohilkhand University and Prof. S.N.H. Jafri, Jamia Millia Islamia, New Delhi for their valuable suggestions and guidance. Lastly, words fail when I endeavour to express my thanks to Dr. K.R. Gupta, Chairman, M/s Atlantic Publishers and Distributors, New Delhi for bringing out this book in a nice form.

**Sudhir Kumar Arora**

# Contents

*Preface*   *v*

1. The Novelist in the Making   1

2. The Thematic Colours and Woman   10

3. Possession: Traditional Image of Woman   35

4. Person: New Woman in the Making   73

5. An In-depth Analysis of the Image of Woman   99

6. Woman through Narrative Techniques   119

7. An Overview   127

*Selected Bibliography*   140

*Index*   146

# The Novelist in the Making    1

The post-Independence era marks the grand inception of the literary emancipation of women. It evinces the creative release of the feminine sensibility, which, notwithstanding its relatively later manifestation, merits recognition by virtue of its self-sufficiency. There germinates an opulent and convincing crop of women novelists in the *terra firma* of Indian fiction in English in the post-Independence era. Several highly talented and prolific women novelists including Kamala Markandaya, Anita Desai, R.P. Jhabvala, Nayantara Sahgal, Attia Hosain, Santha Ram Rau and Shashi Deshpande have enriched Indian fiction in English. Their chief contribution consists of their exploring the moral and psychic dilemmas and repercussions of their women characters along with their efforts to cope with the challenges and achieve a new harmony of relationship with themselves and their surroundings. Kamala Markandaya stands at the head of these women novelists both chronologically and qualitatively.

Born in 1924, Kamala Purnaiya whose *nom de plume* is 'Markandaya' comes of an affluent aristocratic, rather orthodox Tamil Brahmin family of Mysore, South India, where from time immemorial her grandparents and their ancestors inhabited. She could not remain at one place peacefully because of the frequent transfers of her father who was in the railways. Though it was quite wearisome and worrisome, it proved to be a boon affording opportunities to learn more resulting in adding new dimensions in the vast store of her knowledge.

"My father," Kamala Markandaya writes, "was an inveterate traveller and something of a rebel; leaving the traditional preoccupations of his family, he had joined the railways, so that not only was the whole of South India opened to me during childhood and adolescence, but also a good part of England and the Continent.... I think the role of observer which every traveller assumes is good training for any writer.... It makes a good starting point, and I believe it was my starting point."[1]

This early training that she acquired from her father's transferable job worked out miracles in formulating her viewpoint and understanding of man and his life, which stood in good stead in her Olympian career as a novelist.

After a short period of early education in Mysore at the age of sixteen, she joined the Madras University in 1940 where she studied History but left it without completing graduation for the sake of writing and journalism in which she was much interested. She graduated much later in her career. She took up the job of an army liaison officer for a very short period but bade final *au revoire* to it in favour of launching her career as a freelance journalist in Madras and Bombay. From 1940 to 1947, she worked as a journalist and also published short stories in Indian newspapers.

In 1948, she migrated to England where she made a futile effort to get a job of journalist. Ultimately, to support herself, she worked as a proofreader, as a secretary in some private firms and in some other equally dull and soul-killing jobs. Pure gold comes forth from the fierce fire, so did Kamala Markandaya. After confronting the conflagration of adverse circumstances, she emerged with a lot of experiences as a woman who felt and examined the afflicted condition of women. She had settled in England since the age of 25 and married with Bertrand Taylor. She left for Heaven on Sunday May 18, 2004 at her home in the outskirts of London leaving her daughter Kim Oliver behind her.

Like Wordsworth's skylark that soars high in the sky without loosing sight of nest, Kamala Markandaya though settled in England, never loses her touch and affinities with the soil of India particularly South India. Her experience as an expatriate enabled her to acquire a first-hand knowledge of the British policy of colonialism and imperialism. In order to have a first-hand knowledge of rural life, she lived in a South Indian village and observed minutely the life of villagers. "The emerald hills of South India, in full bloom with rice sprouting thrice a year, left a deep imprint on the heart of Kamala and were dearer to her than misty landscape of Wales or light blue azure of the Mediterranean Sea."[2]

No one can escape from the history that works upon the people who draw breath during the time and also builds the firm basis for the time of life to keep pace with time aiming at future. Kamala Markandaya is no exception of this. In her girlhood, she was deeply touched by the ravages of 2nd World War and felt the fervour of the freedom fighters during the Quit India Movement of 1942. She found India awakening, enjoyed the unforgettable moments of freedom of India and also with her weeping eyes, witnessed the massacre at the outset of the partition of the country into two—India and Pakistan. It was impossible for her to remain untouched by the up surging wave of nationalism. During the war, she worked for the army in India and later returned to journalism. Directly or indirectly, she participated and contributed a lot in kindling the fire of patriotism through her career of journalism. She valued Indian traditions and culture more than those of the West. Moreover, she highlighted the anguish of Indians. S. Krishnaswamy writes:

> She, however, is not a theorist to dwell upon caste and class problem only. Her concerns being predominantly socio-economic, her novels offers a savage tale of brutality, ignorance, mental and physical bludgeoning that the ordinary Indian man and woman, is subject to.[3]

Primarily a housewife in real life, Kamala Markandaya herself was conscious of the gender differences when she entered her journalistic career. She had a feminist dread that her domestic duties would stifle her literary career. She expressed this fear when she addressed the European branch of ACLALS in 1975 and mentioned that the book appears one year later in the case of woman writer, as "she has also had to make some 1500 cups of tea and coffee in the meantime."[4]

Kamala Markandaya shot into an enviable prominence soon after the publication of her first novel *Nectar in a Sieve* in 1954. The favourable response from the reading public stimulated her gusto to plug in the cherished direction and every succeeding novel that she penned went on adding new feathers to her cap. The novel became Book-of-the–Month Club Main Selection and bestseller in the United States. In 1955, the American Library Association named it a Notable Book. Her *Two Virgins* made her a literary maestro of international repute as she was given the coveted Asian Prize in 1974 for the book that has been branded as replete with exoticism. She has to-date ten novels to her credit: *Nectar in a Sieve* (1954); *Some Inner Fury* (1955); *A Silence of Desire* (1960); *Possession* (1963); *A Handful of Rice* (1966); *The Coffer Dams* (1969); *The Nowhere Man* (1972); *Two Virgins* (1973); *The Golden Honeycomb* (1977) and *Pleasure City* (1982).

The centripetal force in these novels is India, racked by confusion, violence, economic disparity, convulsive social and political changes. She presents East and West in her works but she seems to have undertaken the task of interpreting the East to the West. "She treats of the theme of tragic waste, the despair of unfulfilled or ruined love, the agony of artistic ambition, the quest for self-realization and truth by the young, all themes popular with European and American novelists of recent decades (Camus, Saul Bellow, Updike).[5]

Kamala Markandaya comes to the fore with firm determination to carry on her fight for the oppressed women in male-oriented society. She has succeeded in studying woman thoroughly. Being a woman, she inherits innate propensity to delve on the plight of women. She perceives their wretchedness from a sociological and psychological perspective. She delineates their dilemma in the form of rootlessness and crisis of identity: a desire to be treated not only as someone's mother but also as a liberated individual. Throughout her novels, her consciousness of what it is to be a woman, both as a member of society and as an individual, emerges as one of her instinctive and passionate concerns. Applauding this quality, Dr. A.V. Krishna Rao observes: "Kamala Markandaya's novels, in comparison with those of her contemporary women writers, seem to be more fully reflective of the awakened feminine sensibility in modern India as she attempts to project the image of the changing traditional society."[6]

Being a woman novelist, Kamala Markandaya has brought mostly women characters into being. As the woman consciousness is central to her world, it is but natural that her key characters should be women. She has created authentic female characters—flesh-and-blood characters with recognizable credentials. She has successfully delineated their problems and plights, yearnings and aspirations, failures and foibles. In comparison of the other Indian-English women novelists, she has won the battle for her women protagonists and has come out with flying colours to be the Victor Queen in the domain of feminine world. She breathes life in her women characters who with the strength of adaptation, convert the challenge of life into a pursuit of finer values that make life worth-living. Her women like Rukmani in *Nectar in a Sieve*, Anasuya and Lady Caroline in *Possession*, Sarojini in *A Silence of Desire*, Mira, Premala and Roshan in *Some Inner Fury*, Helen in *The Coffer Dams*, Jayamma and Nalini in *A Handful of Rice*, Saroja and Lalitha in *Two Virgins*, Mrs. Pickerings and Vasantha in *The Nowhere Man*, Mohini and Usha in *The Golden Honeycomb* and Mrs. Tully and Mrs. Pearl in *Pleasure City* are nobler, wiser, stronger and better than their male counterparts.

Kamala Markandaya uses novel as a befitting medium to reveal different facets of the image of woman and has shown her own self-definition and her emphatic identification with her characters. It is true to some extent that she, despite her strongest pretension to objectivity and high imaginativeness, is subjective and autobiographical, as she has derived nourishment for her novels from life as observed and experienced by her.

Her women characters like Rukmani, Mirabai, Sarojini, Anasuya, Helen, Vasantha, Saroja seem to have been fashioned after the various facets of her crystal clear personality.

Kamala Markandaya scans a conflict between two sets of values, that is, between supremacy of social hierarchy and emergence of the individual. At times it resolves itself into two issues: duty to the family and personal fulfilment. Personal fulfilment is a goal for an individual in Western society. But, in Indian society, fulfilment of oneself at the cost of duty to the family is unaccepted in traditional set-ups. The women characters in the Indian novels are portrayed in the likeness of sacrificing and suffering characters of Sita and Savitri. This is in contrast to the Western novel where focus is laid on the personal happiness of the Individual or the achievement of selfhood or personality. Kamala Markandaya has searched a via media through the New Woman who seeks self-fulfilment through self-expression. The development of her women characters is along moral and spiritual lines which means commitment to a system of values, the longing for a life of fulfilment where fulfilment comes when the woman has a value system and there is also present an environment in which such values can find expression through sharing and participation. Her feministic approach is of co-operation not of confrontation, as she knows that there is no replacement model and ultimately a woman has to merge herself in this male world.

Kamala Markandaya is wonderfully realistic because of her amazing acquaintance with the rural and urban life of the Southern part of India. It is laudable indeed that in the wide spectrum of her novels, she has successfully culled almost all the important aspects and multi-coloured flowers from the bower of human life viz., family life of poor persons in *Nectar in a Sieve* and *A Handful of Rice*; husband-wife relationship in *A Silence of Desire*; exploitation of man by man in *Possession*, *The Coffer Dams* and *Two Virgins*; racial conflicts in *Some Inner Fury* and *The Coffer Dams*; love for country's freedom in *Some Inner Fury* and *The Golden Honeycomb* and a spirit of love and fraternity between the people of the East and the West in *Pleasure City*.

Gifted with a rare literary bent of mind, Kamala Markandaya has got maturity with experiences in life. Social concern is in her blood. Her talent is best expressed in her capacity to explore the vital, formative areas of individual consciousness that project the image of cultural change and in her uncanny gift of inhabiting the shifting landscapes of an outer reality with human beings whose sensibility becomes a sensitive measure of the inner reality as it responds to the stimulus of change.

"Women are natural storytellers,"[7] says Dr. K.R.S. Iyengar and Kamala Markandaya is nothing if not a brilliant storyteller. Her stories are gripping, all absorbing and extremely readable. Readers feel spell-bound and time ceases for them as they are lost in the world of Kamala Markandaya who carries them into an enchanting world where they meet all sorts of men and women who make them realize of their sufferings and teach them how to live and let others live.

It is alleged that her novels lack depth and profundity, as they do not present the novelist's vision of life. It is only partially true. To get pearls, one has to go into the depth. Ideas are not floating on the surface but are lying in the inner layers. The sea churning is indispensable to obtain nectar. On the surface, there is simply a story but under the garb of this simplicity, there is a meaningful message and a vision. She is required a careful reading and one has to rethink while making her final appraisal. It will be injustice to her if one thinks that as a novelist, she is a nowhere woman strolling between the Indian-English literary tradition and the tradition of British literature. Going through and searching something fresh in them, the new face of Kamala Markandaya emerges. She appears to be another Tennyson—a compromise seeker. Like a true saint, she displays the soul of the East to the West. Though she does not belong to either tradition outright English or Indo-Anglian, she lies somewhere in between. However, she prefers India and her culture to the Western culture. Notwithstanding her western upbringing and strong affiliation with England, her soul, her heart, her spiritualism-all are Indian.

Her mastery over English language has won critical applause. Realistic dialogues encompassing almost the entire gamut of human emotions have come out from her pen. "Her language flows, even and beautiful, like the Ganga in the plains."[8] Her prose style, characterized by chastity and lucidity, economy and preciseness, crispness and raciness, displays her felicity and feel for right words and is always highly effective. It achieves poetic heights as she presents the scene of nature, specially flood and drought, the spectacles of hill and natural beauty, the scene of Holi festival and love-relationship.

Kamala Markandaya is the most gifted woman novelist. Niroj Banerji writes: "Her novels are as crystal clear as the water of a hilly lake. There is, undoubtedly, a kind of classical clarity and transparency about them. The novelist does not get lost in the meanderings of a Joycean Ulysses; she rather emerges sure and successful with each successive fictional narrative. This speaks of the continual growth of her mind and art which alone can ensure her a permanent rank among the major fiction-writers of Commonwealth Literature."[9]

Nayantara Sahgal, herself a distinguished novelist says:

> But among the Indian authors I have read...I haven't read all their books.... I am very partial to Kamala Markandaya.[10]

Stephen Ignatius Hemenway praises her highly: "She is definitely one of the most productive, popular and skilled Indo-Anglian novelists and a superb representative of the growing number of Indian women writing serious literature in English."[11]

Though her earlier novels project the traditional image of woman, her later novels, with the changes in time and circumstances, protrude a new face with the renewal of her traditional image. Due to conflicting forces of tradition and modernity, she comprehends the crisis of value adaptation and her attachment with the family. She is at the crossroad. She does not wish to say good-bye to the traditional image. That is why, she searches a via media that leads her towards compromiser. Reaping the crop of traditional image, she sows the seeds of new woman (improved variety of traditional image) that sprout gradually in her novels. But, these seeds that grow in the field of Kamala Markandaya, are matured into a fine crop, which is reaped in the novels of Anita Desai, Nayantara Sahgal, R.P. Jhabvala and Shashi Deshpande.

## Notes and References

1. Montgamery Truth, *Kamala Markandaya* (Wilson Library Bulletin Biography, 1965), 296.

2. Ellena J. Kalinnikova, "The Hindu Woman From London: Kamala Markandaya", *Indian-English Literature: A Perspective*, 149.

3. "Kamala Markandaya: Autonomy, Nurturance and Sisterhood of Man" *The Woman in Indian Fiction in English* (New Delhi: Ashish Publishing House, 1984), 162.

4. Kamala Markandaya, "One Pair of Eyes: Some Random Reflections," *The Literary Criterion*, XI (4) 19.

5. H.M. Williams, *Indo-Anglian Literature, 1800-1970, A Survey*, (O.L.) 84.

6. Rao, A.V. Krishna, *The Indo-Anglian Novel and The Changing Tradition*, Mysore Rao and Raghvan, 1972, 55.

7. Iyenger, K.R. Srinivasa, *Indian Writing in English*, 435.

8. Uma Parmeshwaran, *A Study of Representative Indo-English Novelists*, 54.

9. Niroj Banerji, *Kamala Markandaya: A Critical Study*, 25.

10. Sahgal Nayantara, 'Landmarks', *Span* August 1972, 13.

11. Stephen Ignatius Hemenway, *The Novel of India* (Vol. 2: The Indo-Anglian Novel), Calcutta: Writers Workshop, 1975, 52.

# The Thematic Colours and Woman

## 2

Women have significant place in Kamala Markandaya's novels. Her investigation and presentation of feminine consciousness are directed towards an objective account of women's emotions, assessing Indian womanhood's confrontation with male reality. There is no exaggeration in calling her novels as feminine or womanly as they reflect more the world of women and their ways of life than the world of men. The obvious fact is that her novels breathe in the open atmosphere which is vital for woman and inhale pure oxygen that emits from the evergreen forest belonging to Kamala Markandaya, who herself a woman, treats woman not as a member of society only but as a liberated individual who is searching the possibilities of her own identity in the male-oriented and patriarchal society. She investigates the actual social and emotional bonds that shackle women.

Kamala Markandaya shows her sagacity in launching female characters as her protagonists. Her protagonists possess life-affirming qualities. By making them central characters of her novels, she has highlighted their roles in present-day world. Even the novels that do not have women as the protagonists, receive strength and vigour from female characters. H.M. Williams opines that Kamala Markandaya has, "particular interest in analyzing women characters and suggesting the unusual poignancy of their fate. The narrators are likely to be female, and even when not, the novel will be told mainly from a woman's viewpoint."[1]

In her novels, the female perspective is pronounced in the narrative strategy, be the narrator a woman character in the novel or the author herself. The narrative pattern varies in keeping with the narrator's individual frame of mind and her respective socio-cultural background. Often the narration turns into a process of living through ideas. The narrator's relative position and distance in the textual space, coupled with her exposure to others' experiences and others' points of views, specially the male, work to discipline her own sensibility and thoughts. Her initial viewpoint widens in the associated process of knowing. In the course of narration, the author emerges though not always, as 'drishti', one who sees well.

The wide spectrum of her novels is tinged with feminine colour viz., Socio-economic, Socio-political, Socio-psychological, Socio-religious and Socio-ecological. These colours encompass heterogeneous themes like the theme of tragic waste and despair, of unfulfilled love, of East-West conflict, of psychological maladjustment and social disintegration. They reveal her as a novelist of sensitive and ethical concerns. Kamala Markandaya like a magician, takes these five colours —Socio-economic (Earth), Socio-political (Fire), Socio-psychological (Air), Socio-religious (Water) and Socio-ecological (Sky) to create her female characters.

*Nectar in a Sieve, A Handful of Rice, Some Inner Fury, Possession, Two Virgins* and *Pleasure City* reveal Markandaya's deft handling of the Socio-economic colour. This remarkable colour has different shades, viz. hunger and degradation, tragic waste and despair.

In *Nectar in a Sieve*, Kamala Markandaya has innately shown the soul-breaking appeal of the socio-economic colour. It is responsible for the tragedy in the life of Rukmani who with her pertinacious courage endures it in the monstrous form of Nature's antagonism and expeditious industrialization. The crushing blow of rural life lies in the fact that the people live in the hanging phobia of uncertainties. They are entirely parasite on nature with her innate uncertainties and freaks of the weather. Rukmani says: "Fear, constant companion of the peasant. Hunger, ever at hand to jog his elbow should he relax. Despair, ready to engulf him should he falter. Fear; fear of the dark future; fear of the sharpness of hunger; fear of the blackness of death" (83).

Owing to the natural calamities that result in the failure of the harvest, the tenant farmers find themselves on the edge of starvation and bitterly taste utter poverty that compels them to sell what they have in their possession in order to pay the rent. These words of Rukmani have come out from the core of her heart and express not only her injured feelings but also of the thousands of poor Indian peasants who have to part with their small possessions.

> This hut with all its memories was to be taken from us for it stood on land that belonged to another. And the land itself by which we lived. It is cruel thing, I thought. They do not know what they do to us. (137)

Nature blitzes Rukmani and Nathan first in an irate form of heavy rains resulting in flood and then in the worst form of drought. It destroys everything, leaves nothing to eat and leads to ruin and despair. The equation MORE RICE TO SELL changes into NO RICE TO SELL and in the end, into NO RICE TO EAT.

Kamala Markandaya's remarkable quality that sets her off from other Indian-English novelists is her realistic approach to literature. She presents veritable replica of hunger before her readers and makes them feel of the afflictions of the villagers as an independent observer. Rukmani voices their feelings:

> For hunger is a curious thing, at first it is with you all the time, waking and sleeping and in your dream, and your belly cries out insistently, and there is a gnawing and pain as if your very vitals were being devoured, and you must stop it at any cost, and you buy a moment's respite even while you know, fear the sequel. Then the pain is no longer sharp but dull, and this too is with you always, so that you think of food many times a day and each time a terrible sickness assails you, and because you know this you try to avoid the thought but you can not, it is with you. (91)

"Hunger," in the words of Hari Mohan Prasad, "appears like an octopus in the novel. It is the real evil stronger than the original Satan that disturbed the bliss of the Eden garden."[2]

Hunger shows Kunthi the safest path of prostitution and later on lures her to blackmail Rukmani and Nathan so that she may save herself from starvation. The python of hunger swallows Poor Old Granny and makes a false promise to Ira that it will not touch the life of Kuti, her brother if she sacrifices her chastity. It is, indeed, an irony that in our society such self-sacrifice as was done by Ira to save the life of her brother is neglected and labelled as a sin. People without considering the original circumstances, feel no hesitation in branding such woman as immoral and a stigma on the fair countenance of the society.

A hungry man is an angry man who knows no law, commits crimes and debases himself by facing the world through questionable means. Nothing allures him except bread and to get it, he becomes ready to do anything as his noble qualities and moral considerations, for the time being, are dried up. Ravi in *A Handful of Rice* is no exception of this and it is he who represents the people who are surmounted by the devil. Ravi, having no control over his hunger, enters forcibly the house of Jayamma who asks him what he wants.

> What do you want?
> Food, I told you, he said impatiently,
> And be quick. (7)

K. Radha rightly points out that *A Handful of Rice* begins and ends with the hero's struggle to procure food with the little money he has, Ravi drinks in order to forget his sorrow. He tells Apu, the tailor, "I'm starving. I'm hungry. I want a meal." Apu's wife hits him with all her force for breaking in like a ruffian and blood drips from his face. "I was hungry," he explains. Hunger had forced him to leave his village where people lived "between bouts of genteel poverty and acute poverty".... Poverty made him abandon his 'decency.'[3]

It is Nalini who brings a drastic change in his life. He falls in love at first sight. He longs for marriage that will provide solace and mental peace to his agitating mind. He dreams of her and feels elated when he thinks of her.

> If I had a wife, he thought as he ate, she would cook for me, it would like this every day—but what had he to offer to get himself a wife?—I'll buy her a little house, small but nice. (11)

He succeeds in marrying her but fate sends two devils—poverty and hunger to shatter his dreams. Poverty and hunger take the life of his dear son Raju and incite him to beat innocent Nalini. The worst follows when out of frustration and anger, he rapes his own mother-in-law Jayamma.

Socio-economic colour is traceable even in *Some Inner Fury*. The upper class people who have food more than enough, leave plenty of it after every meal. This food is the dream of many hungry children who are standing outside waiting to pounce on any crumb, which they may take. Kamala Markandaya presents this real picture in moving words:

> So they waited, watchful even while they played, brown wily urchins with the warped bodies of perpetual hunger, and the bright uncomplaining eyes of children who somehow contrive to ignore it. (*Some Inner Fury* 92)

Premala has sympathy for such starving children and her heart moves at their pitiable plight. Kit is indifferent to their pitiable condition and never broods over it like Premala. He believes that the more one helps them, the more they come.

Socio-economic colour is sprayed in dots on the scenery of *Possession* that relates the piercing story of a father who sells his son Val for five thousand rupees to Caroline who makes him dance according to her tune. It is poverty that makes Val's father forget of his relation with his son for the sake of money. It also seduces him to think of Val as a commodity that will bring a lot of money. Val's mother knows her husband's nature very well. She says:

> He has already decided. Did you not hear him? It was the money—it was too much for him. But it is always

so, men are ever free and easy with that for which they have neither suffered nor laboured. (*Possession* 20)

In *Two Virgins*, Kamala Markandaya leaves the beaten track of degradation that poverty and hunger bring. She presents the new face of degradation, which is the result neither of hunger nor of poverty. Rather, it is the outcome of a fashion of the modern society, which claims to be advanced. The craze to be modern, to look modern and to think like modern lures Lalitha who becomes an easy prey to the allurement of Satan that appears in the pleasing shape of Mr. Gupta. Mr. Gupta, a film director, exploits innocent girls for satisfying his lust for the white flesh. He transgresses when he says to Lalitha's father, "I am not made of stone" (*Two Virgins*, 220). Chingleput whom Saroja takes as her guide dupes and shocks her sense of morality and trust. He turns into a beast and takes advantage of her innocence. 'Fair faces with ugly desires' are the proper words for such mean men.

In *Pleasure City*, the description of the fishing colony that has come under the influence of modern materialistic civilization is pathetic and heart touching:

> Day after day the catch turned out poor. They ate so meagerly; the cramps were beginning. These were not unknown, but good seasons made them forget the suicidal, mackerel had spoilt them all. (*Pleasure City* 56)

The fishermen, who are the victims of this new influence, are compelled to work in the Shalimar Complex. Under the impact of materialistic aroma, Mrs. Contractor manages Shalimar and takes care for enjoyment. Even Valli also serves as a sales girl in Shalimar Complex.

None can deny socio-economic factor that is indispensable for existence. Its excess or scarcity mostly leads to degradation. Yet, economic colour cannot be discarded. Without it, one cannot breathe to live; and breathe one must with it. Kamala Markandaya's female characters are badly affected as they feel its need everywhere.

Kamala Markandaya had undergone the disastrous experiences and hardships of the National Movement. She could not remain unaffected by it emotionally and imaginatively. Yet her vision always remained objective and positive. Dr. R.S. Singh is of the opinion that she is "to a large extent unbiased and balanced; her aim is to display how various attitudes and ideologies shaped the human destinies in the context of the British regime in India."[4]

In fact, it lent socio-political colour to her novels with kaleidoscopic casts and nuances. *Some Inner Fury*, *Possession* and *The Golden Honeycomb* very well expose political tension, upheavals of nationalism and patriotism.

*Some Inner Fury* is, undoubtedly, a fury against the British people who oppressed the Indian people during the struggle for Independence. The Indian people are shown fully involved in freedom movement boycotting the foreign goods. Mira describes Govind's attitude towards the Western influence on India:

> Govind was not and had never been a part of it. To him it was the product of a culture which was not his own.... For those who had participated in it he had a savage harsh contempt. (*Some Inner Fury* 121)

Kamala Markandaya rightly brings out the picture of the Indian society, which was coloured with political consciousness. The political conflict between the Indian patriots and the British rulers was an external aspect. Even the members of a family could have divergent conflicting views on various aspects of political struggle. It was a scene of people who were extraordinarily political alive. Govind believes in violence whereas Mira and Kit's wife, Premala, are in favour of peaceful means to oppose the cruel British rulers.

Showing her ardent nationalism and her utter identification with, and, approval of the Quit India Movement, Kamala Markandaya presents a graphic description of the conditions of India under the British rule:

> All day the city was full of whispering. There were rumours, murmurs and mutterings of little faith in courts of conspiracies; of men who were jailed for and

the wind of discontent would pass from end to end, from quarter to quarter, and every little alley and side-street would be alive to its message. This is the price you pay, if once you have sought to circumscribe freedom. (*Some Inner Fury* 265)

Roshan, who sacrifices her parents, her husband and the aristocratic life for the sake of her motherland India, symbolizes the liberated woman of modern India. When Govind is tried in the court on the charge of murdering Kit, Mira who loves Richards decides to leave him because he belongs to the community of rulers.

In *Possession,* Caroline's possession of Val symbolizes the Britishers' attempt to 'possess' India. The British do their best to exploit the people, but the strong spiritual values keep the *esprit de corps* of the Indian very high and, finally, they hit *coup de maitre* to remove the Britishers from India. Caroline, who is conscious of the conflict between India and England, succeeds in inspiring Val to start painting work by sending him forged letters in the name of the Swamy. She tells Anasuya:

> Do you know, we go out of our way to meet, and we squabble every time we do. It's a sort of love—hate relationship, don't you think? Like the kind Britain and India used to have. (*Possession* 169)

*The Golden Honeycomb*, which deals with the struggle for Independence, reveals the evil design of the cunning British Rulers who deftly play the foul game of politics. It is a story of three generations of Rajas of an erstwhile princely state of Devapur. Bawajiraj II is installed as the Raja of Devapur in the British controlled India. His son Bawajiraj III is provided such education as alienates him from his own people. After his father's death, he becomes the ruler of Devapur but remains constantly under the watchful eyes of the British Resident. He is forbidden to make treaties. But, his son Rabindranath who is a true patriot defies his father for being a yes man of the British political Agent. He tells Sir Arthur, the Resident: "My birthday's the day Victoria died. No body wanted her to be. She became Empress by conquest; the people never wanted her" (70).

What Jijabai did for Shivaji, Mohini does for Rabindranath. Usha with her mesmeric personality bewitches Rabi and makes future plans with him. Kamala Markandaya has boldly referred to the callous attitude and barbarous behaviour of the British imperialists towards Indians. They had their own axe to grind. But Indians should not forget that they have their long heritage of ancient ideals and values, which they should keep up; at the same time, they may not hesitate to imbibe the best from the west if any. This is the message she conveys.

Kamala Markandaya is at bay in imparting socio-psychological colour to all her novels. Unlike Mulk Raj Anand and other Indian-English fiction writers, she has endeavoured her best to present how diverse shades of socio-psychological colour affect the strings in making or marring human relationship, how sundry desires of giving and receiving love are not translated into action and remain unfulfilled and how the lack of mutual understanding leads to frictions and social disintegration. "As an artist, Kamala Markandaya," says S. Krishnaswamy, "sincerely believes in the universal sisterhood/brotherhood of man and that her writing systematically espouses the cultivation of warm, caring human relationships cannot be denied."[5]

In the world of *Nectar in a Sieve*, Rukmani, Old Granny and Dr. Kenny are the ideals and pleasant shades of socio-psychological colour whereas Kunthi and Biswas are the patterns of nauseous shades. Rukmani is the ideal character that plugs in the links of human relationship with others. Where human relations are based on selfishness, love and feelings play no role. Ira's husband forsakes her, as she is sterile.

> Mother-in-law, I intend no discourtesy, but this is no ordinary visit. You gave me your daughter in marriage. I have brought back to you. She is a barren woman. (*Nectar in a Sieve* 54)

Rukmani departs to meet him when Ira is cured of her sterility. But, she is shocked to discover that he has married another woman. Ira's husband says:

For she was a good wife to me, and a comely one, but I have waited long and now I have taken another woman. (*Nectar in a Sieve* 65)

Rukmani's husband Nathan is not thoroughly devoid of moral sense as he has consciousness to confess his guilt before her. He confesses frankly his relations with Kunthi. This is the spirit that glues sound and healthy relationship. When Nathan dies, she feels alone and desolate in the wide world.

Rukmani and Nathan provide the complete freedom of choice to their sons who are growing up. They never blame when Arjun and Thambi are turned out of their jobs. Nathan tells Kali in an angry tone: "Our children must act as they choose to, not for our benefit. Is it not enough that they suffer?" (*Nectar in a Sieve* 70)

Dr. Kenny, who dedicates his life for the cause of humanity, is the Messiah to Rukmani and the family. Kunthi, who commits countless sins, does not hesitate to blackmail Rukmani by threatening her to disclose to Nathan her liaison with Kenny. She does not spare Nathan and blackmails him too by threatening to disclose his illicit relations with her own self. It is sweet and amiable Old Granny who partakes of joys and sorrows of Rukmani as a family member. Rukmani feels fidgety when she thinks of the future of Ira. Then, Old Granny consoles her saying: "Why fear? Am I not alone and do I not manage" (*Nectar in a Sieve* 66). Her sacrifice can be seen when she gives the only rupee left with her to Ira's child. She died of starvation and her death leaves a deep imprint on the heart of Rukmani.

Some people exploit the poor and needy by honeyed tongue and take undue advantage of their pitiable plight. Biswas, the bania belongs to this category. He tempts Rukmani by purchasing her vegetables at a much higher rate than she expects, thus causing injury to the old woman who dies of starvation.

In *Some Inner Fury*, national movement alters the psychology of the characters and deeply influences their ways and attitudes. Kit, a thoroughly westernized Indian, fails to make a healthy relation with his wife Premala—whose roots are in Indian culture. Being an Indian to every inch, Govind, though cousin of Kit reveals his contempt for the British. Mira, an Indian, loves an Englishman Richard who poses to be an Indian. 'The Quit India Movement' divides the loyalties of the people by its fury. It does not allow Mira and Richard to meet and with the gush of antipathy and racial tension creates two separate banks that never meet.

In *A Silence of Desire*, Sarojini who goes to meet a Swamy for the cure of her growth i.e. tumour without taking her husband, Dandekar into confidence, gives birth to suspicion in his mind. He loves her deeply and insists her for an operation but she shows her staunch faith in the cure of the Swamy. Dandekar, with the help of his officers, succeeds in turning the Swamy out but he is obsessed with a sense of guilt. In this victory, he remains a loser and develops the feeling that he is inferior to the Swamy. The socio-psychological colour of human relationship leaves a message that husband should confide in their wives and should not suspect without any proof. It is reciprocal understanding that is needed to maintain a healthy relationship between husband and wife.

In *Possession*, Caroline Bell, who is the representative of exploitation of the poor by the rich, discovers the talent of painting in Val. She buys him from his parents, takes him to England and makes him a source of making money and satisfying her sexual lust. The insatiable thirst for money makes Val's father forget his relation with him. Val's ideal is the Swamy and he seeks his permission before going with Caroline. He is shocked when he comes to know about the forged letter and also her selfish motives. He realizes that Caroline is responsible for turning Ellie out of the house as she cannot bear his relations with any other girl. She has injected poison into the ear of Annabal by telling her about his illicit relations with Ellie and her subsequent suicide. He feels so disgusted that he returns to India to live with the Swamy. Caroline comes again to reclaim but, this time, he refuses as he does not wish to be possessed by her.

In *A Handful of Rice*, Kamala Markandaya has shown that hunger and poverty have psychological effect on human relations. Ravi, who comes to the city with a dream, is disillusioned and becomes a prey to the underworld. He longs for a decent life but poverty, as an obstacle, always hinders his way. Poverty and hunger make him lose his balance of mind. One night, he beats his wife Nalini and in a fit of anger, rapes his mother-in-law Jayamma. The death of his son Raju shatters him and he goes to meet Damodar, who rejects him detecting him of no use. Nalini is the only lady who supports her husband Ravi and tries to understand him. She does her best to pacify him.

> You are getting high and mighty; putting yourself on a level with high-class folk. How can we ever be like them? Why can't you be content with what we have? (*A Handful of Rice* 75)

In *The Coffer Dams*, Clinton, who fails to feel the Indian sentiment, symbolizes the hatred of the Christian towards the non-whites. Human feelings do not matter him. Helen, who represents those healthy forces that are active to develop healthy relation, tells her husband Clinton:

> It's nothing to do with age. I just think of them as human being, that's all. You've got to get beyond their skies, darling. It's a bit of hurdle, but it is as essential one. (*The Coffer Dams* 12)

She mocks at Clinton's indifference to human feelings and says to him:

> Don't human beings matter anything to you? Do they have to be a special kind of flesh before they do? (*The Coffer Dams* 105)

The British and the Indian officers look down upon the hill-tribesmen. But, Helen does not think like them. It is she who crosses the gulf of caste, colour and culture and believes only in one religion—religion of humanity based on love and fellow feelings.

*The Nowhere Man* is a psychological study of human relations, which are weakened by the racial conflict. Srinivas, who regards England as his native country, becomes a victim of this racial conflict, as the young men hold non-whites responsible for the depression in economy. Now, he feels that cordial relations are only a dream. He realizes that if he leaves England, he has nowhere to go.

> Nowhere, he said to himself, and he scanned the pale anxious eyes which were regarding him out, a nowhere man looking for a nowhere city. (*The Nowhere Man* 174)

His wife Vasantha is shocked and dies leaving him alone. Laxman marries without her consent and even does not call his mother Vasantha on the occasion of the birth of a baby. Mrs. Pickering, a poor old divorcee, has a kind attitude towards Srinivas and helps him in his emotional isolation. Mrs. Fletcher, mother of Fred, feels repentance for the misdeeds of her son and consoles Srinivas: "Mr. Srinivas, you belong here, and don't let anyone convince you different" (*The Nowhere Man* 174)

V. Rangam rightly observes that "this novel treats of larger human relations rendering the work an interesting psychological study of human relationship as well as of the essential loneliness."[6]

In *Two Virgins*, there are characters like Mr. Gupta who, knowing the psychological weaknesses of some of the innocent girls like Lalitha, exploit them to their advantages and kick them when they are of no use for them. Lalitha, who is lured by the glamour of the modern world, falls a victim in the hands of Mr. Gupta, the film director, who exploits her sexually. When she realizes the fact of her pregnancy, she decides to commit suicide but is stopped by her younger sister Saroja. Even after such a bitter experience, she leaves her parents for good, as she is unable to resist the lure for the modern life. It is Saroja who is firm and steadfast and does not move before the masculine allurements in the form of Devraj or Chingleput.

To have possession forcibly on another's land gives birth to anger and hatred. This is the psychological colour that is on the canvas of *The Golden Honeycomb* with different shades of racial tensions and hatred of the people. Rabi opposes his father Bawajiraj who is a puppet in the hands of the British rulers. Mohini kindles fire in him to make him ready for the freedom struggle. Usha co-operates him, inspires him and never lets him feel alone in this battle. Anil Bhatnagar writes in this connection:

> This novel of Kamala Markandaya clearly conveys the message that human relations are based on the feeling of unflinching love and the sense of identifying oneself with the sufferings of the people irrespective of status, creed and birth.[7]

In *Pleasure City*, Kamala Markandaya has shown that there is nothing to stop East and West to come closer if one approaches with love and affection. Tully, an English officer of the AIDCORP acknowledges Rikki's perception of beauty and his honesty. There is a feeling of fraternity that is running in the fishing community. Mrs. Bridie does her best for the welfare of the people of the fishing colony. She shares in their joys and sorrows. She belongs not to a particular country or a community but to the family of human beings. Rikki makes relations not on selfish motive but on the basis of bonds of humanity. He presents a flower to Tully as a token of love. He tells his sister Valli. "He is as human as you or me" (*Pleasure City* 73). Rikki builds a boat, which is a symbol of love for Tully in his heart.

Kamala Markandaya's acumen lies in mixing the socio-psychological colour and then brushing it on the canvas of her works. Going through the picture gallery of her works, one can meet the characters that are painted in natural colour exhibiting their ways, tastes, attitudes, perception and fulfilled or unfulfilled desires. Her most praise-worthy quality, which is not in other Indian-English women novelists in such degree, is her magic of sketching a real character that, neglecting the dual dealing theory, expresses his/her inner beauty and the reader can easily make an accurate estimate without falling into the error of conjecture.

In *Nectar in a Sieve, Possession* and *A Silence of Desire*, Kamala Markandaya has superbly painted the socio-religious colour that includes different shades—fatalism, superstition, material versus spiritual values etc. Though she shows her indifference declaring them merely passive ones, she cannot help herself without appreciating their plus points that enable the Indian people to face the hardships of life patiently without blaming anyone. Kamala Markandaya, in an article, writes: "I am astonished at the peasant Everyman's stupefying degree of endurance and resignation."[8]

The Indian people, who are coloured in socio-religious feelings, are stoic and, hence, resign to their fate without weeping and lamenting. With the passage of time, they develop endurance for unimagined sufferings. In *Nectar in a Sieve*, Rukmani and Nathan face untold sufferings but like a stoic they bear them. Rukmani, who longs for a son, actually bears a daughter. But, she consoles herself by thinking that Gods are very busy and cannot attend to everyone. Being religious to every inch, she presents her daughter Ira, a small lingam that is a symbol of fertility.

> Wear it, you will yet bear many sons. I see them, and what the dying see will come to pass...be assured, this is no illusion. (*Nectar in a Sieve* 22)

Believing in 'Hope sustains life,' she feels a sense of relief with the little rice that she has. For tomorrow and unborn future, she dreams of eating fish, earning some money and having a sound sleep. She has firm faith in God's mercy.

> We are all in God's hands and He is merciful. (*Nectar in a Sieve* 54)

Due to Dr. Kenny's treatment, Ira becomes free from the curse of sterility and is now fit to be a mother. Nathan goes to Ira's husband to convey this good news. But to his shock and surprise, he finds that he has married another lady. Nathan and Rukmani again resign to the will of God. Rukmani tells Nathan:

> No fault of yours, or the girl's or her husband's. It is fate. I do not like to think of the future. (*Nectar in a Sieve* 66)

When the rain fails, there remains nothing. Once again, Rukmani tries to please God.

> I took a pumpkin and I wept at her feet. I thought she looked at me with compassion and I went away comforted, but no rain came. (*Nectar in a Sieve* 76)

But, her prayers remain unanswered. When Dr. Kenny sees the sufferings of Rukmani's family, he scolds her for having such religious feelings. But Rukmani defends them and consoles him.

> Do not concern yourself. We are in God's hand. (*Nectar in a Sieve* 133)

The Indians believe in Swamies who, in their opinion, are the representatives of God. In the novel 'Possession', Val who goes with Caroline, asks for the permission of the Swamy and the gods in the cave before leaving

> ...while I am there I can see my gods, so it will be two things done. They are all there in the cave. I want to take leave of them before I go. (*Possession* 23)

With Caroline, he is restless and unsatisfied as the Swamy always comes on the screen of his conscious mind. When she comes to possess Val once again, she meets the Swamy who enlightens her thus:

> There are temples, churches, cathedrals...men have put all they possessed into their building and adornment but the name of the creators are lost—yet even you, lady Caroline, would not look on it squandered labour. (*Possession* 231-32)

We feel the victory of spirituality over materialistic comforts when Val decides to stay with the Swamy. K.R. Chandrasekharan rightly remarks:

> The struggle between the Swamy and Caroline for the control and custody of Val truly becomes symbolic of the struggle between the Indian spiritual values and Western materialism for the art or even the soul of India.[9]

In *A Silence of Desire*, Sarojini's faith in the healing powers of the Swamy is incontrovertible. She believes to the extent that the tumour in her womb will dissolve if he touches her head. She spends her days at his Ashram and her nights in solitude and prayer neglecting her house, her children and daily routine. She is the representative of the religious minded Indian women who better believe in the Swamy's healing power than medical treatment. Though the Swamy does not claim to be a healer, every person who meets him, returns with a peace of mind. After the departure of the Swamy, Dandekar asks his wife what she intends to do without him. She says:

> Nothing, what should I do? I formed an attachment, it is broken, that is all. One must accept it.... It would be sinful to batter oneself to pieces because one refuses to recognize that another's life is his own. If the Swamy chose to go, it was his decision. One must accept it in good heart. (*Silence of Desire* 217)

Thus, Kamala Markandaya succeeds in lending different shades of the socio-religious colour to her novels. She believes that stoicism provides the Indian people a sort of mental strength and protects them from the danger of tension and conflict.

Lastly, socio-ecological colour can be discerned in the world of Kamala Markandaya's novels. Her novels are a study of plantation of characters on such lands as are quite different and alien to their nature and environment. Kamala Markandaya is fully acquainted with the east-west conflict, rootlessness, the problems of the immigrants and racial antagonism. Generally her novels, in the opinion of C.D. Narasimhaiah, "reflect her strong penchant for Indian values as against the spiritual impoverishment of English society but Indians are not spared. Actually her good men and women come from both cultures."[10]

While delineating different shades of this colour, Kamala Markandaya shows no favour either to the east or to the west. She is quite intelligent as she looks at the west through the eyes of the east and she looks at the east through the eyes of the west. Nathan and Rukmani in *Nectar in a Sieve* are the representative of the East while the speedy industrialization and Dr. Kenny represent the West. Dr. Kenny, who loves the Indian people, feels disgusted with their follies, poverty and silent humility. Although he consoles Rukmani in her sorrows yet he scolds her stoicism.

> Times are better, times are better. Times will not be better for many months. Meanwhile you will suffer and die, you meek suffering fools. Why do you keep this ghastly silence? Why do you not demand—cry out for help—do something? There is nothing in this country. Oh God, there is nothing! (*Nectar in a Sieve* 47-48)

He shows no interest in the Indian philosophy of fasting for the purification of soul. "My God! I don't understand you. I never will. Go, before I too am entangled in your philosophies" (*Nectar in a Sieve* 116). But he does his best to improve the lives of the Indian people as he collects a large sum of money from England for the construction of a hospital in Rukmani's village. Passive and submissive are the proper words for the people of the East while active and conscious of their rights are for the people of the West. But, it does not mean that Kamala Markandaya is in favour of the West. Rather, she brings out the strong points of the Eastern culture. Marriage, in the Western culture is simply a contract, but in the eastern culture, it is not a contract but a sacred relation. Dr. Kenny says: "My wife has left me. My sons have been taught to forget me." (*Nectar in a Sieve* 111).

The foundation of the world of *Some Inner Fury* is the feeling of hatred, which has kept the east and the west apart from meeting. Kitsmay, an Indian trained in Western culture and Govind, rooted in Eastern culture are anti-poles to each other. Mira, who sacrifices her love during the trial of Govind, loves Richard, who tries to bring India and England closer by imbibing the Indian culture. The fire of hatred dries up the river of heart and human values are turned into ashes. The innocent persons like Premala and Hickey come with the buckets of sympathetic water to throw on it but it takes them in its grip and swallows them.

Indian spiritualism and Western modernism are in conflict with each other. Dandekar in *A Silence of Desire* thinks that his wife Sarojini is deceiving him by going to a Swamy's house daily in order to get her tumour cured. It is against his wishes, as he wants to get cured through a surgical operation by a qualified surgeon. This creates a wide gulf in their relationship and gives birth to an emotional tussle between them. C. Paul Verghese rightly observes:

> This conflict between the husband and the wife is treated in the novel as part of a conflict between science and superstition. The novelist in presenting the conflict does not make an outright condemnation of superstition or faith healing Swamy. She attempts to strike a balance between science and superstition.[11]

In the end, Sarojini agrees for the operation as the Swamy allows her. She tells Dandekar: "I am not afraid now of knives or doctors, or what they may do. All will be well. He said so." (*A Silence of Desire* 218)

The needle of Sarojini's strong faith pricks the suspicious balloon of Dandekar and the air of Western philosophy comes out. Through her, the author also makes us aware of the tensions inherent in a confrontation between Eastern and Western attitudes towards religion, suffering and man-woman relationships, herself having been a witness to it all.

In *Possession*, Caroline Bell who symbolizes Western materialism tries to possess Val who represents Indian spiritualism. As spiritual values are deep-rooted in Val, he gets success in liberating himself from the clutches of Western materialism. Kamala Markandaya makes Anasuya assert:

> Possession. I thought appalled: attenuated form of the powerful craving to have, to hold, which was so dominating and menacing a part of Caroline; which left grey and ugly trail of human misery such as, horribly swollen but not unrecognisable, one saw stumbling in the wake of power societies and empires. (*Possession* 217)

Caroline describes her relation with Val saying: "We go out of way to meet, and we squabble every time we do. It's a sort of love-hate relationship, don't you think? Like the kind

British and India used to have" (*Possession* 70). She says nothing when Val stops painting due to his new relation with Ellie. Her relation with Val, she says, is "the classic ailment. That England and India never did understand one another" (*Possession* 77). When she accuses the Swamy of exploiting Val, the Swamy remarks: "He works for that and therein is the glory; it gives men a satisfaction so rich they cannot explain it and mostly they don't even wish to" (*Possession* 232).

*A Handful of Rice* deals with the age long conflict between oriental and occidental cultural values. The West holds in abomination Eastern traditions and ways and in return, the East depreciates Western styles and modes. Kamala Markandaya has very judiciously presented both sides of the coin. She thinks that the Westerners hold in abomination the Eastern ways and traditions while the Easterners depreciate their styles and modes. If the author denounces the wantonness and immodesty of the West, she appreciates their punctuality and regularity. Similarly if she decries leisurely adoption of life's ways by the East, she applauds its humility and modesty. She does not like priggishness and conceit of the Europeans. Very slyly, she makes a sarcastic remark on their shamelessness:

> Ravi had sisters and so he knew the strict watch that was kept on young unmarried girls in their community, in all communities except shameless ones like the Europeans. (*A Handful of Rice* 40)

Kamala Markandaya sees life steadily and sees it whole avoiding all artifice, sentimentality and straining after effect. She is conscientious in representing reality and holds the balance as long as possible and thus she is able to set up both the sides.

Ravi is lured by the glamour of modern life in towns. He becomes a prey to various vices and falls in the hands of the underworld King Damodar and his men. But, the soft emotional touches of Nalini provide some relief and he comes out of the mud to live peacefully but this modern world under the impact of Western modernism deprives him of the oxygen that is necessary for existence and gives him carbon dioxide in the form of hunger and starvation.

In *The Coffer Dams*, socio-ecological colour is painted with the contrasting shades of technological and human level. On the technological level, the conflict lies between the technological power and the forces of nature represented by the turbulent—South Indian river on which the dam is being built and also the heavy rains which try to obstruct the construction work. On the human level, the arrogant British officers, like Clinton and the poor hill tribesmen who are working as labourers, are in direct conflict. Helen, wife of Clinton is the only lady who has soft corner for them. She scolds Bashiam for not rising against injustice done to the tribal people who were forced to leave their lands. Krishnan tells Helen about the passiveness and absence of integrity among the tribal people.

> The British had eaten it away during the centuries when they were the rulers and Indians ruled; it would take a century to form again. (*The Coffer Dams* 71)

All human beings are equal. Kamala Markandaya through Helen expresses her own views on the equality of men. "It is nothing to do with their age. I just think of them as human being, that's all. You've got to get beyond their skins, darling. It's a bit of hurdle, but it is an essential one." (*The Coffer Dams* 12)

Quite contrary to Helen is another British lady, Millie Rawlings who is deadly against Indians, "Never trust the blacks. That's my motto and I stick to it." (*The Coffer Dams* 37)

Clinton adopts the dual policy of the western culture as he suspends the work to provide Baily and Wilkins a decent Christian burial while he decides to continue it without considering two tribesmen's dead bodies, which could not be traced because of jamming of a boulder. He wants to achieve his own goal of completing the dam even if the bodies are incorporated into the structure. Hence, there is an inherent conflict in the outlooks of the east and the west. Kamala Markandaya believes that mechanical progress is meaningless if it is achieved by suppressing human values.

In *The Nowhere Man,* the young men of England like Fred, Mike, Joe and Bill feel that the black are depriving them of their jobs. Fred who is full of bitter gall against them gets so angry that he challenges a coal black man sweeping the streets:

> Here, you. You have got no right to be in this country. You bugger off, see. (*The Nowhere Man* 171)

But the Blackman replies to him in the same coin. "I got my right when you lot carved my country." (*The Nowhere Man* 171)

However, exception is everywhere and this exception is Mrs. Fletcher, mother of Fred. She entreats Srinivas not to leave England and asks him to treat it as his own country. Srinivas, in fact, is the representative of thousands of Indians and other Asians who are living in England and have become the victims of racial conflicts. Srinivas shows not only his wounds but their wounds also.

> I am to be driven outside, which is the way they want it. An outsider in England. In actual fact I am, of course an Indian. (*The Nowhere Man* 242-43)

He faces the tragic fate when Fred burns him to death as a result of cruel racial conflict. However, all are not like Fred. There is a group of people like Dr. Radcliffe, Mrs. Pickering, Mr. Glass and Mrs. Fletcher who have kept up the image of the West.

There is also a difference between the East and the West on the cultural level. The eastern Vasantha is a devoted wife who is always at the beck and call of her husband whereas the western Dr. Radcliffe's wife ignores her husband and is not wholly devoted to him as the former is. In Indian culture, parents are looked after with love and care in their old age but in the Western culture, this notion does not exist. Srinivas' son Laxman who is born and brought up in the Western culture, forgets the sacred bond of love between parents and children. He selects a girl for himself without the consent of his parents and leaves his parents alone in their old age to their cruel fate.

The grounds of traditional simple village life and the artificial modern city life are different in nature and values. In

*Two Virgins,* Saroja and Lalitha represent the traditional simple village life and the artificial modern life respectively. Lalitha, who has a leaning towards modern outlook, is attracted by the glamorous life of the city. Having been exploited by Mr. Gupta, the film director, Lalitha returns to the village but goes to the city once again as pleasures of the modern life attract her.

Appa teaches both the sisters not to discriminate between the Sikh and Hindu but to live as one. "It was British stratagem to divide the people up and set one against another in order to rule them" (*Two Virgins* 11). In the opinion of Appa, the British rulers were nothing but tradesmen who forced people to use only British imported goods. But, it does not mean that Appa is against the Europeans. Appa says: "One must take an overall view. One imbibes what is bad in the West as well as what is good, he said, there are no national frontiers" (*Two Virgins* 113).

In *The Golden Honeycomb,* Kamala Markandaya has shown that the British rulers look down upon the Indian people and exploit Maharajas for their self-interest. Rabi throws cold water upon their plans and devotes himself in uprooting them. He is well acquainted with the suffering of the poor labourers. "Scores of thousands of people had been disinherited, some of them of their own land, most of them of their spirit." (*The Golden Honeycomb* 251). However, Rabi respects Sir Arthur who is judicious, honest and kind towards Indians. He makes friendship with Sophie, Sir Arthur's daughter. This shows that he is against the English rulers for their cruel way of ruling the country.

In *Pleasure City,* Kamala Markandaya hopes that if a better spirit of understanding and co-operation is developed, it will result in harmonious relations of the East and the West. The friendship of Rikki and Tully shows a ray of hope and reveals the fact that there is not yet end of the dream of bringing the East and the West together. The face of a far removed fishing village in South India is transformed as the Indian Government decides to build a holiday complex to be called Shalimar. The work is given to the Atlas International

Development Corporation. Shalimar comes into being and leaves impressions on those who come in its contact—Apu, Mrs. Pearl, Carmen, Valli, and Corinna etc. The friendship of Tully and Rikki is the symbol of a friendship of modern and traditional in the changed environment. This relationship is based on co-operation and sincere friendship without the touch of materialistic possessions or master-slave notions.

A close study of the thematic variety of Kamala Markandaya's works provides a glimpse into the female psyche. Her novels deal with a full range of feminine experiences. Her women dominate the scene and are superior to male characters. What Ruskin said about Shakespeare that 'he has no heroes but heroines,' is quite true in case of Kamala Markandaya who has portrayed almost every form of woman. Her skill of painting the portraits of women with different colours, viz. Socio-economic, Socio-political, Socio-psychological, Socio-religious and Socio-ecological, is laudable. With the alchemy of her art, she has transmuted them into bright stars and her male characters into planets that have no light of their own but receive it from the stars that shine brightly with their own light.

## Notes and References

1. H.M. Williams, "Victims and Virgins: Some Characters in Markandaya's Novels." *Perspective on Kamala Markandaya* ed. Madhusudan Prasad (Ghaziabad: Vimal Prakashan, 1984), 28.

2. *The Fictional Epic on Indian Life*—A Study in Theme and Technique of Nectar in a Sieve", *Perspective on Kamala Markandaya* ed. Madhusudan Prasad (Ghaziabad: Vimal Prakashan, 1984), 99.

3. K. Radha, "The Hunger and Anger of Ravi in Kamala Markandaya's A Handful of Rice", *The Indian Journal of English Studies*, Vol. XXX, 1991-92: 14.

4. "Soulful East and Ratiocinative West," *Indian Novel in English—A Critical Study*: (1977), 14.

5. "Kamala Markandaya: Autonomy, Nurturance and the Sisterhood of Man" *The Woman in Indian Fiction in English*, 167.

6. "The Nowhere Man: A Critical Analysis," *Perspective on Kamala Markandaya*, 186.

7. *Kamala Markandaya: A Thematic Study* (New Delhi: Sarup and Sons, 1995), p. 114.

8. "Reminiscences of Rural India," *Galbraith Introduces India*, ed. John Kenneth Galbraith (New Delhi: Vikas, 1974), 109.

9. East and West in the Novels of Kamala Markandaya," *Critical Essays on Indian Writing in English,* ed. M.K. Naik (Dharwar: University of Dharwar Publications, 1977), p. 330.

10. "Other Indian Literatures—English," *Comparative Indian Literature,* Vol. 2 ed. George (Madras, Macmillan, 1985), 1302.

11. "Indian English and Man in Indo-Anglian Fiction," *Indian Literature,* Vol. 13, 1.

# Possession: Traditional Image of Woman

## 3

The Indian system, with a few exceptions, is specialized by patriarchy, which identifies male dominance and female subordination. The leading role is in man's share and woman who has to be satisfied with the secondary role, remains in the background. She is expected to mould herself in the pattern of the family into which she is married and merged her individual identity into that of her husband. She becomes her husband's shadow and follows him through the course of life. She is expected to support him in all kinds of weathers, adding her strength to his. Chastity and devotion to her husband are her precious ornaments. Family is her shrine and the enclosure in which she remains confined, is Kitchen where she operates her daily activities like cleaning, washing, cooking etc. In bedroom, she worships her husband and calling him her 'Pati-Parmeshwar', as he is not less than God for her, she offers flowers of worship at his feet at night. She observes several fasts to ensure the same husband life after life. She also prays for the long life of the husband so that she does not have to suffer the sufferings of the widow.

The Kitchen culture that she inherits from her mother brings decency, decorum, order and fragrance. She knows fully well that, in future, she has to be the Kitchen Queen of her so-called sweet home. This is the traditional image that a girl forms in her mind in girlhood. She is taught to be submissive, committed, docile and tolerant so that she may prove herself an ideal woman not only for her husband but also for her father-in-law, mother-in-law and other-in-laws. She is supposed to keep the family tree grow and prosper. She is taught not to copy male qualities that will make her polluted and demonic.

> Man for the field and woman for hearth
> Man for the sword and for the needle she
> Man with the head and woman with the heart
> Man to command and woman to obey.[1]

Marriage is a woman's adventure and with it, there is an end of her search as she merges herself in the family losing her identity. Now, for her, family becomes more important than individual. She sacrifices herself following the merging and self-negating theory. She wishes to produce a son to continue the pedigree. The infertility, she knows well, is a curse. S.C. Dubey has significantly analyzed it.

> The infertility of a woman was considered as a curse, in patrilineal groups she is expected to produce a son to continue the line. In matrilineal societies this was not considered a necessary, though it was desirable. But even among them, as in patrilineal societies, procreation is a social necessity and a value.[2]

Leela Dubey observes: "For woman, the positive value of marriage, which signifies "good fortune and a state of bliss," is contrasted with the negative and inauspicious significance of the widowhood."[3]

A traditional woman, being deeply religious, develops stoicism that gives mental potency and protects her from tension and conflict. And it is true that happy women do not make history. Suffering women make it and epics are the records of suffering women.

Kamala Markandaya projects her women characters basically traditional women with all their characteristic traits and inborn qualities. She is conscious of the silent barriers that are laid against women.

> There is a tradition. Perhaps not only in India, that women should not be worried, that the best way to ensure this is to keep them as far as possible in ignorance.... Certain domains belong to men alone, and

Indian women learn early not to encroach. (*Some Inner Fury*, 117)

She laughs at the ways of 'society, the beastly tamer'; when she says:

All the rules and restrictions against which you had chafed since you were a little girl, all were designed, it was amply confirmed as you grew older, to stop you becoming pregnant until the marriage be not had been tied. It did not work. (*Two Virgins* 136)

Social institutions like marriage and family, Kamala Markandaya believes, emotionalize human relations. Marriage, for her, seems to be a symbol of community and marriage in her world is the final resting place for a woman. Her early novels present the wife in her customary role of Sati-Savitri archetypal pattern. But, underlying this suffering sacrificial role is the new woman who complains with pressing tongue for emancipation.

Kamala Markandaya's *Nectar in a Sieve* is the story of Rukmani who never loses faith in life or love for her husband and children—despite her endless battle against relentless Nature, changing times and dire poverty. Praising Rukmani, A.V. Krishna Rao observes:

The real truth of the novel is the spiritual stamina of Rukmani against such formidable enemies to her culture: the draconian landlord, and the soulless industry. She knows:

Work without hope draws nectar in a sieve
And hope without an object cannot live.

And this mother of Rural India lives in her children, Selvam and Ira who belong to a different age but who are of the same self.[4]

Rukmani, the youngest of her sisters—Shanta, Padmini, Thangam is the daughter of a village headman who, due to changing circumstances, is forced to marry his daughter to Nathan, a tenant farmer who is poor in everything but certainly not in love. Being the protagonist of the novel, she adopts the dramatic role of a sad chronicler of the traditional life of an Indian village in transition.

As soon as the marriage ceremony is over, she leaves her father's home with her husband Nathan in a bullock-cart. This memory is still fresh in her mind. She reviews of past:

> Then the cart began to move lurching as the bullocks got awkwardly into rhythm I was sick. Such a disgrace for me…. How shall I ever live it down? I remember thinking. I shall never forget…. I have not forgotten, but the memory is not sour. (*Nectar in a Sieve* 9)

She feels the soft touches of her husband who soothes and calms her saying: "It is a thing that might happen to anybody," he said. "Do not fret. Come, dry your eyes and sit up here beside me" (*Nectar in a Sieve*, 9). On reaching her new home, she sinks down as much with grief as with deep anguish and frustration. I wanted to cry. This mud, nothing but mud and thatch was my home. My knees gave first the cramped one, then the other, and I sank down" (*Nectar in a Sieve* 10)

But her husband assures her that very soon they will have a better and bigger house. She is deeply touched by his kindness and can never forget it. She assures him that the house is all right and she is happy with him. She does not complain at all and is rather grateful to her husband for being so kind to her. Love starts showering in her heart when she comes to know that Nathan has built the hut with his own hands for her. The mud house is the creation of love and so she admires her husband for his nobility of heart. She feels highly euphoric and proud realizing the intensity of her husband's love. She says:

> A woman they say always remembers her wedding night. Well, may be they do; but for me there are other nights I prefer to remember, sweeter, fuller, when I went to my husband matured in mind as well as body not as a pained and awkward child as I did on that first night. (*Nectar in a Sieve* 8-9)

It is not on the first night but later that she comes to love him as a true and dutiful wife. She is faithfully devoted to her husband and according to Indian traditions, does not call his name but addresses him only as 'husband':

It was my husband who woke me—my husband, whom I will call him Nathan for that was his name, although in all the years of our marriage I never called him that, for it is not meet for woman to address her husband except as "husband" (*Nectar in a Sieve* 9-10)

Being a sagacious and prudent housewife, she manages her home well. She is amiable and gentle and soon she has a number of friends among the womenfolk of the village. She is particularly close to Janki and Kali, though she does not like Kunthi so much. However, when Kunthi gives birth to her first child, she serves her to the best of her ability, though it puts so much of strain on her. To increase the family income, she sows some vegetables in the small patch of ground at the back of the cottage. She sells first to Old Granny and then to Biswas, the banya, as he pays a much higher price. She collects cow dung early in the morning from the fields around, and thus saves the cost of purchasing fuel. She is prudent and farsighted and even in days of prosperity saves something for the rainy day.

She gives birth to her first female child and names her Iravadi. But after that she does not conceive for full seven years. Her husband wants a son to carry on his name. He waits patiently but she feels his pain and disappointment. At her mother's house, she meets Dr. Kenny and confides her troubles to him. It is by virtue of his treatment that she conceives again and soon becomes the proud mother of six sons—Arjun, Thambi, Murugan, Raja, Selvam and Kuti. She never tells her husband about the treatment that she has taken from Dr. Kenny.

Her concept of life is very simple and elemental; it does not require being much happy. She ponders on bare necessities consisting largely of food, clothes, and shelter.

While the sun shines on you and the fields are green and beautiful to the eyes and your husband sees beauty in you which no one has been before and you have a good store of grain laid away for hard times, a roof over you and a sweet stirring in your body, what more can a woman ask for? My heart sang and my feet were light as I went about my work getting up at sunrise and going to sleep content. Peace and quiet were ours. (*Nectar in a Sieve* 12-13)

She is a keen observer of nature. She believes that Nature represents some cosmic power—constructive and destructive. She expresses her point of view:

Nature is like a wild animal that you have trained to work for you. So long as you are vigilant and walk warily with thought and care, so long will it give you its aid, but look away for an instant, be heedless or forgetful, and it has you by the throat. (*Nectar in a Sieve* 43)

The happiness of Rukmani and her family is dependent on good harvest and that in turn is dependent on timely and adequate rains. Nature plays the game of 'hide and seek' and ultimately snatches all joys from her life-destroying the crop—sometimes in the form of heavy rains—sometimes in the form drought.

She does not get over the shock given by Nature. Meanwhile, industrialization in the form of tannery flattens her. She is quite aware of this chance. "But the change that now came into my life into all our village, blasting its way into our village, seemed wrought in the twinkling of an eye" (*Nectar in a Sieve* 29).

She is dead against the change because of its noise, stinking smells and crowds. In place of quiet, the village has "all noise and crowds everywhere and rude young hooligans idling in the streets and dirty bazaars and uncouth behaviour and no man thinks of another but schemes only for his money" (*Nectar in a Sieve* 50). The tannery, symbolizing industrialization and its associated evils, invades the village with clatter and din, depriving it of its children's playground and raising the bazaar prices high. With the setting up of tannery, she feels that the crows, kites and other scavenging birds that are eager for the filth and garbage of the town, have taken the place of paddy, bird and flamingoes. She pathetically recollects:

Somehow I had always felt the tannery would eventually be our undoing. I had known it since the day the carts had come with their loads of bricks and noisy dusty men, staining the clear soft greens that had once coloured our village and clearing its cool silences with clamour. (*Nectar in a Sieve*, 135)

But, she does not wholly hold the tannery responsible for her misfortunes. Her husband is dispossessed of the land on which he worked for thirty years under the illusions of owning up. Her poignant words, which are spoken nostalgically, describe the pathetic plight of an uprooted farmer.

This home my husband had built for me with his own hands in the time he was waiting for; brought me to it with a pride which I used to better living, had so very nearly crushed. In it, we had lain together and our children had been born. This hut with all its memories was to be taken from us for it stood on land that belonged to another. And the land itself by which we lived. It is a cruel thing, I thought. They do not know what they do to us. (*Nectar in a Sieve* 137)

She is shocked when her son-in-law returns Ira saying that she is a barren woman. She knows that people think a barren woman to be a counterfeit coin, which is returned to the owner or discarded, as useless. Her sorrow crosses all the limits when she discovers Ira who has been prostituting to buy milk for her ailing brother Kuti. She tries to stop her daughter but of no use as she has made up her mind that she will neither go hungry herself nor allow her brother to do so. Her helplessness is seen in these lines.

Well we let her go. We had tried everything in our power; there was nothing more we could do. She was no longer a child, to be cowed or forced into submission but a grown woman with a definite purpose and an invincible determination...we forbade, she insisted, we lost. So we got used to her comings and goings as we had got used to so much else. (*Nectar in a Sieve* 103-04)

A woman can bear a shock but her husband's infidelity, is too much for her. She faces the gravest crisis in her married life when she learns about her husband's relationship with Kunthi. She is stunned as she thinks of Kunthi who continues blackmailing her for Platonic relationship with Kenny. First she is speechless, later full of speech.

"Disbelief first; disillusionment; anger, reproach, pain. To find out after so many years, in such a cruel way.... At last I made an effort and roused myself:

"It is as you say a long time ago," I said wearily, "That she is evil and powerful I know myself, let it rest." (*Nectar in a Sieve* 90)

She becomes shockproof as one shock comes after another. Death sees her house and carries her son Raja to the unknown world. She reacts to the death of her son Raja thus:

For this I have given you birth, my son that you should lie at my feet with ashes in your face and coldness in your limbs and yourself departed without trace, leaving this huddle of bones and flesh without meaning. (*Nectar in a Sieve* 93-94)

She shows herself spiritually and mentally strong when she says:

...These things were you? Now there is no connection whatever, the sorrow within me is not for this body which has suffered and in suffering has let slip the spirit, by for you, my son. (*Nectar in a Sieve* 93-94)

Nathan tells her that their last child Kuti, conceived in glee have been taken away by cruel Death. She grieves for him and feels too well what Nathan feels. Her grief is more controlled, though no less poignant this time:

Yet, although I grieved, it was not for my son; for in my heart I could not have wished it otherwise. The strife had listed too long and had been too painful for me to call him back to continue it. (*Nectar in a Sieve* 105)

She muses over the death of Old Granny in a philosophical manner:

Death after all is final.... So it had been with my sons so it was now with Old Granny, one day it might be the same for me, for all of us. A man might drift to his death before his time unnoticed...." (*Nectar in a Sieve* 125)

Similarly, when Nathan dies, she says poignantly: "I licked my wet lips. There was a taste on them of salt and of the fresh sweetness of the rainwater. I did not know I had been crying" (*Nectar in a Sieve* 185).

Time is a great healer, and with the passing of time, she reviews her life with "calm of mind, all passions spent." Her calm acceptance of the reality of the situation and stoic resignation to the Immanent Will manifest typical image of an Indian woman. Meena Shirwadkar identifies her with Maurya in J.M. Synge's play, Riders to the Sea.[5] Failures of harvest, the deaths of Raja and Kuti, the departure of her sons for city and for Ceylon, the desertion of Ira by her husband, the withdrawal of Selvam from agriculture, the deprivation of land—all these tragic incidents make her "a Mother of Sorrows"[6] but fail to crush her spirits or to shake her faith in the basic human values. Having faced the biggest blow of her husband's death, she comes back to her village with a renewed faith in an adopted son Puli and reconciles to life, which is in store for her.

*Some Inner Fury* is set against the background during the Second World War when the Quit India Movement was in air in 1942. It studies the impact of the troubled national spirit upon the love of Richard and Mirabai who belong to the different races—the ruler and the ruled. Mirabai is the central consciousness of the novel. She is the most roundly presented character with her sensitivity and imaginative insight. She is more modern than traditional as she is brought up in a westernized household where there are two dining halls and two sets of cooks (one western and the other Indian) and whose members go to European clubs and dance and play. In the family, club going is compulsory for everyone and Mira is introduced to the club to get her adequately Europeanized:

I went because I was taken; and to learn to mix with Europeans. This last was part of my training, for one day-soon—I would marry, a man of my own class who, like my brother, would have been educated abroad and who would expect his wife to move as freely in European circles as he himself did. (*Some Inner Fury* 24)

But her Europeanized mind does not obstruct her from being a traditional woman. She has Indian heart and possesses Indian tolerance and fortitude. At the railway station, she goes to welcome her brother Kitsmay who returns with his English friend Richard from England. It is the tradition of Indian culture that the guest is like a god and hence, the first priority is given to him. She welcomes Richard with the garland that she has brought for her brother. The traditional shyness can be seen on her face when she garlands him. "And yet the first time we met I was so shy I hardly looked up until someone prodded me and I stumbled forward and garlanded him." (*Some Inner Fury* 8)

Her heart is highly exhilarated and feels for him when she sees him trying to imitate an Indian by wearing a dhoti and a pair of chappals that he borrows from a servant. A seed of love starts germinating in her heart. She goes to the club not with her father but with Richard and feels quite cheerful and smiling. A gift from Richard becomes more meaningful to her. His absence makes her uneasy as a chameleon in summer. To be in the company of Richard becomes a pleasure in itself. She shows the vastness of her heart in loving him. It is in the roots of Indian culture that when one loves, loves whole-heartedly and devotedly.

Love or duty, if there is one option to choose out of these two, surely a traditional woman will opt for duty sacrificing love. Country becomes more important than her love and she sacrifices it for the sake of performing her duty. Mira opts the traditional manner. When Richard asks her "Do you really think people can be singled out like that? One by one, each as an individual? At a time like this?—After today?" (*Some Inner Fury* 218).

Mira, in spite of her optimism and bravado, realizes that this is true. She says:

> But it was not; it was just beginning though exactly of what I could not tell.

> There is a time in one's life, they say, when one opens the door and lets the future in: I had the feeling I had done so, but had neither the power nor the courage to recognize the shape of things to come; and therefore I could not speak. (*Some Inner Fury* 218)

Her fears come true when Govind is accused of stabbing Kit to death by Hickey. So, Govind is arrested and put on trial. She is convinced that Govind is innocent since she remembers that she had thrown her arms around Govind as Kit left the hut, and therefore it is impossible for him to have thrown the dagger. Hickey maintains that he had seen Govind throwing the dagger. Before the issue could be decided, the court is mobbed by slogan-shouting crowds and Govind is taken away. She also realizes that it is no longer possible for her to keep herself aloof from her own people and maintain her relationship with Richard. She rises above the self and plunges into the great redeeming fire of the national movement. Quite helplessly and inescapably, she forsakes her love reconciling her lot with the crowd. After all, she is convinced:

> ...it was simply the time for parting we had known love together, whatever happened the sweetness of that knowledge would always remain. We had drunk deeply of the chalice of happiness, which is not given to many even to hold. Now it was time to set it down, and go. (*Some Inner Fury* 285)

She takes the great decision of leaving her lover for the sake of her country. Country is bigger and higher than love for her. She is not mean and selfish as she thinks of the people and the country.

> Go? Leave the man I loved to go with these people? What did they mean to me, what could they mean, more than the man I loved? They were my people those other were his...and I know I would go, even as I know

Richard must stay. For us, there was no other way, the forces that pulled us apart were too strong. (*Some Inner Fury* 285)

H.M. Williams calls this love, "a deep and maturing experience for both young people, is shipwrecked on the rocks of Indian nationalism."[7] The influence of the idealistic national movement is so far-reaching and unrelenting that it prompts K.R. Srinivasa Iyengar to regard *Some Inner Fury* 'a tragedy engineered by politics.'[8]

The floods of the Quit India Movement engulf this love of Richard.

Comparing Mira with Rukmani, Laxmani R. Moktali says:

If her heroine Rukmani in *Nectar in a Sieve* represents the peasant women folk, Mirabai of *Some Inner Fury* represents the rebellious young blood of pre-independent India. If one is rural, the other is urbane. But the situations in which these women are placed, are more or less, the same, in that both of them had once their golden days and are now thwarted. The problem is universal. But, the environment is particular, that is peculiarly Indian.[9]

Quite opposite to Mira-Richard relationship, which is based on love without marriage, is Premala-Kitsmay relationship, which is better known as marriage without love. Premala, who is traditionally brought up, lives in a world defined by her parents and society. She is made to deny her impulses and is forced to live according to an abstract set of ideals far removed from reality. Her family has protected her from the realities of being a woman. Her mother wishes Kitsmay to be her son-in-law but he will not marry Premala until or unless he meets her. In order to facilitate marriage, Premala comes to stay with Kit's family. She knows, of course, the object of her coming. "No woman, after all, goes lightly to her marriage, there are always shadows before" (*Some Inner Fury* 51)

When she comes, she is quite nervous and her face becomes wet. She feels uncomfortable in the new changing circumstances as Mira says: "She (Premala) is too young. I thought, forgetting she was older than me. To me she seemed a child and this feeling was always to remain for like a child, she had no defences" (*Some Inner Fury* 52).

She is by nature shy and conventional and basically Indian in spirit. She bends backwards in order to become a suitable mate for Kit; she endeavours to mould herself according to his ultra modern tastes. She comes to Mira to borrow her shorts, which she puts on only to satisfy Kit's likings. But her blushing has no meaning and favour in the eyes of Kit.

> ...for she would have done anything for him—Premala came to borrow my shorts, put them on, blushing: blushed again, furiously, when Kit looked at her bare legs, for she had never worn anything but a sari. But this modesty, which is supposed to grace a woman, found little favour in Kit's eyes. (*Some Inner Fury* 53)

During a month, she wins everybody's heart in the family. There was no one who could not speak of Premala with affection, "for she was gentle and unassuming, and had tender pleasing ways" (*Some Inner Fury* 55). Mira who likes Premala praises her saying: "And Premala...? A lovely face, tenderly moulded, which never lost its tenderness because she could never learn to be tough" (*Some Inner Fury* 143). In her heroic efforts to please her husband and abiding by the concept of dharma, she thinks nothing of abnegating her identity. She is deeply religious and is in accord with the religious part of the ceremony. Mira writes about her religious nature.

> Several times I saw her praying eyes closed, forgetful of the crowd, with that expression of desperate entreaty you sometimes see on the face of a small pleading child. (*Some Inner Fury* 72)

Within a year of her married life, she and her husband drift apart. She is Indian to the core and cannot adjust completely to Kit's lifestyle—though not for lack of effort on her part. She has sympathy for the children who are fighting for scrapes. As she sees their pitiable condition, she is moved to pity. Dodamma and Kit are against this sentimentality and ask her not to be sentimental. She says: "It is neither emotional nor sentimental to call children children" (*Some Inner Fury* 63). She is innocent, modest, utterly unpretentious and universally loved. "To her, goodness of heart was almost the sum of perfection and little else of consequence: for there are many keys that unlock the gates of men's liking, and each is differently fashioned" (*Some Inner Fury* 155).

She becomes a martyr without a cause. She sacrifices herself at her attempts to be an ideal wife and later when she rushes to protect the school, which she has helped to build, and which to her perhaps symbolizes the reason for living, she is burnt to death. Govind blames Kit for driving her to her death.

> "She loved you," he said, "You never loved her—you do not even know the meaning of love. You gave her nothing not even a home. You drove her to the village— you drove her to her death." (*Some Inner Fury* 240)

Premala remained virtuous and beautiful in her life and also in her death, she was looking more beautiful. Death who would not have the courage to touch and destroy her beauty, helped a lot in making her more beautiful. Mira writes about her death: "But I could not believe she was dead. The feeling would not come, then I looked at her and she had always been beautiful and she was beautiful now" (*Some Inner Fury* 239).

For people like Premala who scatter love around, death means nothing because one remains beautiful in death. Premala as her name suggests, is an embodiment of love—prem and she, like a reformer, must lavish on her husband, on Govind, on the adopted child as also on the entire village but which, in the pervading violence and hatred, cannot survive and must inevitably die.

Kamala Markandaya's rare gift to scrutinize human crises of a fundamental strain and to track grippingly and realistically the psychological stress and isolation is no better seen anywhere than in her novel *A Silence of Desire*, an imaginative commentary on the psychological mal-adjustment of a middle-class woman Sarojini who is religious and traditionalist to the core. Sarojini's husband Dandekar, a clerk in the New India centres his whole peaceful life on his adored wife, his love for her and three children. Though she knows no luxury, she is quite satisfied with what she has and builds the building of her sweet home on the foundation of mutual confidence. But, one evening by her absence at home, she causes an earthquake that shakes the building. N. Ramachandran Nair observes:

> Kamala Markandaya seems to stress the point that there are times at which one has to keep silence and times at which one has to speak. Indiscretion in this regard may be detrimental to the preservation of joy and peace. Dandekar and Sarojini are victims of such an impasse. The root cause of their prolonged uneasiness is their inability to speak out.[10]

Kamala Markandaya portrays Sarojini calling her "a good wife, good with children, an excellent cook, an efficient manager of his household, a woman who still gave him pleasure after fifteen years of marriage, less from the warmth of her response than from her unfailing acquiescence to his demands" (*A Silence of Desire* 7). The walls of a house reveal the character and nature of the woman who lives among them. The walls of Sarojini's dining room clearly reflect that she is deeply religious. "These were all of gods and goddesses singly and in groups, tableaus that showed them holding court in their heavens, or worrying, or being miraculously born of the earth or the sea" (*A Silence of Desire* 11).

Sarojini, whose life is full of sufferings due to severe ailment is pious and naïve. She spends much of her time in prayers and visiting temple where she listens to the preaching of saints and prophets—swamies. She truly believes that the saint will bring her healing. Her husband Dandekar is modern in outlook but cherishes the traditional image of woman and wishes to see it in his wife Sarojini. He makes others know about his attitude towards woman. "Our women are not like that. They do not flaunt themselves in front of men either before marriage or after. They are brought up differently" (*A Silence of Desire* 24).

But this same Dandekar changes his opinion when he finds Sarojini absent and sees a photograph of a man. She is shocked at her husband's spying on her and takes deeply to her heart when he calls her a 'soiled woman'. Her sense of righteousness arises, she will state rather than explain.

> The man whom I worship as a god; she said, looking at him directly. You are very nearly right in that one thing. Just that one thing (*A Silence of Desire* 72).

A traditional woman values her chastity above all and thinks it to be 'the precious ornament of her life.' Sarojini thinks that she is right and has done nothing wrong that makes chastity unchaste. She informs him: "I have a growth in my womb" (*A Silence of Desire* 86). This disclosure stuns him as he thinks the worst: it could be cancerous. To his whispering "If only you had told me...why could you not tell me?" (*A Silence of Desire* 87). She replies that he would have called her superstitious, a fool and then reasoned with her until she lost all faith.

> Because you would have stopped me going to be healed.... You would not have let me be—no! You would have reasoned with me until I lost my faith, because faith and reason did not go together and without faith.... I shall not be healed. (*A Silence of Desire* 87)

Their intimacy begins to reassert itself; it does not matter if it is temporary. Both make their emotions flow out as soon as they find an outlet. Sarojini is more emotional than her husband.

> I didn't mean it—She was gasping for words, for breath —did not mean what I said. Anger makes you say— strange things, but I did not mean—how could I?—after so long and—and our happiness, but it wasn't—wasn't me. (*A Silence of Desire* 88)

Her husband persuades her to have an operation but she refuses flatly.

I can't
'I will be cured, in my own way.'
'By this—this faith healer?'
'Yes, I have faith in him and he will cure me.' (*A Silence of Desire* 108)

She finds herself under pressure but she is capable of keeping poise even in the adverse circumstances. Significantly, she does all possible to keep the home going. She works hard and sleeps as little as possible to compensate for the time she is away. Her explanation that the Swamy has left is direct, free of rancor, though, obviously deeply distressing to her. She gets the strength of her character and tells her husband Dandekar:

> "I formed an attachment, it is broken, that is all. One must accept it.... He prepared us for his going, I realize that now though I didn't at the time...perhaps because I did not want to. He said there must be no repining," she said, "He was insistent on that." (*A Silence of Desire* 217)

She becomes ready for an operation, as she has got inspiration and strength from the Swamy. "I'm not afraid now of knives or doctors; or what they may do? All will be well. He said so. Her face was confident" (*A Silence of Desire* 218).

Truly, in *A Silence of Desire,* there is more 'silence of speech' than 'silence of desire.' Both Sarojini and Dandekar lack mutual understanding and they almost do not speak. At last, this dumbness of the couple is broken and everything becomes all right. Sarojini decides to entrust her life to medicine and successfully undergoes an operation. She recovers and is now free from the power of Swamy.

Kamala Markandaya's another prominent novel *Possession* deals with the story of a traditional woman but in a different cast. She is the central character, yet her friend Anasuya who is only a minor participant in the action narrates the story. Hence, the story is told predominantly from Indian point pf view. Iyengar has rightly commented on the role of Anasuya:

> Perhaps Anasuya (or Kamala Markandaya) is trying to make the story of Caroline and Valmiki something of a

parable of colonialism, the passing of one empire, and the current insidious movement of new-colonialism.[11]

Anasuya is a friend of Caroline who comes to India and then takes Valmiki, a young talented Indian, with her to England. She narrates the story as an objective reporter. Her character remains enigmatic to the end, and hence, is the frail bridge between Kamala Markandaya's eastern and western world.

Anasuya is well aware of Indian tradition and her culture. When Caroline, who after discerning in Val the talent of a painter, wants to take him with her, Anasuya makes her remember: "You forget" I said, "He may have a family. He may not want him to leave them. They may not want him to leave" (*Possession* 10). Hence, she refuses flatly to help her. "I meant I was not going to help you. This boy is a human being, even if he's a goatherd and a simpleton. He's not a toy to be picked up now and discarded when something else takes your fancy" (*Possession* 10).

Anasuya feels the pulse of Caroline who does not wish to lose Val at any cost. She analyses her (Caroline's) anxiety for Val and his attachment with the Swamy. She peeps into Caroline's heart and describes:

> I think she saw him as in the end the real adversary the one who could, more formidably than anyone else who had crossed her path, show up for shadows her authoritative declarations of an austere disinterestedness in and a legitimate entitlement to the boy; and resist her taking and keeping possession of what she wanted (*Possession* 104)

Though she is a friend of Caroline, she is deeply impressed by Ellie. "I found it was not she but Ellie who dominated me. Pale ineffectual Ellie, asleep—or more probably awake—in her room across the landing, surrounded by Valmiki's work, and carrying his seed in her womb" (*Possession* 118).

Anasuya is sympathetic, kind and merciful to Ellie whom she sees being exploited by Caroline. She supports Val and is aware of the struggle that is taking place in his mind.

Quite contrary to the Swamy who represents the traditional spiritual image of the East, Caroline Bell represents the traditional materialistic view of the west. What she sees, she sees with the spectacle of materialism. The British traditional face of cruel exploitation emerges in her. She can have her own way for she has the attributes of the British who, wherever they go, "as the whole of the East knows, they live on the fat of the land, though the British themselves have no inkling of it" (*Possession* 14).

She is the representative of her race in her pride, possessiveness, egoism and cunning manoeuvres. While portraying her character, Anasuya says:

> She was supremely confident, born and brought up to be so, with as little though of fallibility as a colonial in the first flush of empire, as a missionary in the full armour of his mission, dogged by none of the hesitancies that handicap lesser breeds. (*Possession* 15)

The desire to taste 'arak', crude country liquor made by villagers, takes her to a South Indian village where she meets by accident Valmiki, a rustic Tamil boy who has natural born talents of a painter. She perceives with an uncanny insight the rich potentialities of Valmiki as an artist. She buys him from his parents for five thousand as compensation for the loss of his services. She succeeds in settling the matter.

> Caroline must have known at once she had won for she put her arm round the boy, as it were taking possession of him in full view of his family. (*Possession* 20)

She takes him to England where she makes him, in the purely western sense of the term, a celebrated painter. Her attitude signifies the changed role of the Whitman's burden to maintain control over others—to substitute political dominance by cultural dominance with a view to alienating Indians from their own roots.

She takes pride in Val and boasts: "I discovered him in a cave. Oh yes, a real one. In India. Hideously bare and uncomfortable, except for those superb walls. And Val of course" (*Possession* 125).

From the very beginning, she is aware of the Swamy's invisible influence on Valmiki. In her eagerness to possess the boy outright, she oversteps the bounds of matriarchal patronage by seducing him into an almost incestuous carnal alignment despite the disparity in their ages and the difference of race. Whenever she fails to get on well with Val, she describes it as an old 'ailment,' "that England and India never did understand one another" (*Possession* 77). When the Swamy visits London at the invitation of International Guild for the Advancement of Theosophy, she remarks angrily: "It's a seduction, spiritual if you like. There's no place for it in England. He ought never to have been allowed in" (*Possession* 143). Her concept of Val's art is 'essentially bourgeois'; she looks at his painting merely as commodities to be bartered in the market rather than an expression of his communion with the divine.

Valmiki for Caroline is a means to achieve success in society. After winning the recognition in the higher society, Caroline aspires for the recognition of Valmiki himself and makes him her lover. Desiring to bind the young man to herself, she does not disdain anything: she forces the Tamil cook to write Valmiki a letter on behalf of his friend Swamy, drives away her maid-servant Ellie who expects a child from Valmiki and thereby drives her to commit suicide, discredits the young man in the eyes of his beloved Annabel, and deprives Valmiki of any means to return to India. Val is her discovery and, therefore her possession. She is the representative of the traditional image of the Britishers who exploited Indians and other people of the world. She stands for those people who "do not easily give up what they think are their possessions" (*Possession* 198).

In Ellie, Kamala Markandaya portrays a 20-year Jewish girl who looks crippled and aged because of the cruel inhumanities she has suffered at the hands of Nazis in concentration camp. She is described as "a victim of European crime in European confine" (*Possession* 73). "A refugee, a domestic last bastion of the servantless era" (*Possession* 71) is Ellie in the opinion of Caroline who supposes her "better than nothing" (*Possession* 71). Being orphan, she is hopeless and helpless.

> She had no parents, no state, no passport, no papers none of those hollow stacking blocks on which the acceptable social being is built. Her one asset was that she was trained and fully experienced domestic help. (*Possession* 72)

She has no particular musical ability, but for music itself she has real love as well as a deep insatiable mind. Anasuya presents her the entire collection of records. Though she refuses yet on pressing, she accepts on condition that she will return them on her return. Caroline refers her saying Poor Ellie and is surprised when Val makes her portrait. She tells Anasuya: "It's beyond me why Val should have thought her worth putting on canvas" (*Possession* 105)

She feels quite easy and comfortable with Anasuya and at her lodging, she plays on music of her liking—Mozart and Handle with the volume so low that the music is reduced to a whine, though even that seems to satisfy her. Anasuya asks her whether she loves Val or Val loves her. She tells her:

> I lie with a man—so I do not talk about love, because I do not know if that is what I feel. It is not easy to feel because I am burnt out, inside. I am burnt out. But Valmiki loves me. He does not know it, but he does. At times like tonight he forgets, he cannot understand himself how it is possible to love someone so dull as I am, you can see in his face he is asking this question. Then when the others are gone and it is day time again he comes back to me, we are of one kind. (*Possession* 116)

She has the seed of Valmiki in her womb. She has the feeling for a child "If I had no feeling for a child would I have conceived?" (*Possession* 116). It is a surprising fact that she was raped every night in the camp but she was not conceived. And she sleeps with Val only once and is conceived. Raping symbolized colonial suppression and her conceiving final inevitable liberation.

"First time with Valmiki," she said carefully, "but in the camp it was every night. They came for us every night. In the beginning I would ask them to kill me but they only laugh...it made it worse." "...I was too dry. Also after a few months were not women any more...the flow stopped, we looked like men no flesh, no hair." (*Possession* 116)

Ellie, an innocent girl becomes a prey to colonial suppression and exploitation. Val is right when he says about her "but she still bleeds within" (*Possession* 84)

Nalini in *A Handful of Rice* is drawn with a masterstroke. She is virtuous, decent and comely with bright eyes and thick glossy hair that could transform a man's life. Her voice is ever soft and low which is an excellent quality in woman. Ravi falls in love with her at first sight and longs to be bound in nuptial bond. He assesses her in following words:

What a girl like that, and half a man's troubles would be over. (*A Handful of Rice* 25)

Haply, Iyengar agrees with him for he says: "What is, however, astonishing is the woman's power of patient endurance, her inexhaustible capacity for love, her simple tenderness. The sisters Nalini and Thangam are the salt of the earth and the character of Nalini is exquisitely drawn. She is the sort that can redeem even an errant husband like Ravi. Fallible he may be, but he does not cease to be a credible human being, always more sinned against than sinning."[12]

Nalini's charm makes Ravi adopt an honest job of tailoring and makes him aware of respectability and "a respectable householder, a decent citizen with a decent job and a wife to support" (*A Handful of Rice* 25). It is the magic of her personality that attracts him to be a gentleman. A.V. Krishna Rao observes: "...Nalini symbolizes the subtle fragrance of life, a clean, healthy and traditional life. She promises "sweet life but demands hard and honest labour."[13]

It is she who becomes a ray of hope in his life and converts his barren life into glistening greenery with the water of sympathy, tenderness, love and affection. "Remove Nalini and

Ravi would be watered down version of Damodar."[14] She is a flesh and blood embodiment of his dream. She gives him a sense of satisfaction, a comfort, in the form of "the sound of her, the swish of her sari as she whisked about the place at her mother's biting, or a glimpse of her sitting cross-legged like an inaccessible goddess in one of the inner rooms" (*A Handful of Rice* 34).

In their quest for happiness of individuals and of the family disregarding social considerations, Ravi and Nalini together become, as Kamala Markandaya suggests, "symbolic of India" (*A Handful of Rice* 189) for Nalini has what Ravi lacks and together complementing each other, they can be very effective where most people in the new generation fail. Nalini has some traces of Apu's uncomplaining temperament, endures poverty, faces other difficulties and puts up with thrashing at the hands of her husband even in the advanced stage of her pregnancy. Ravi sees her fighting for breath, massaging "her abdomen or arching her back for relief against the cold granite stone, but he had never heard her complain" (*A Handful of Rice* 195).

Hers is stoic ungrudging attitude towards the 'sea of troubles.' In fact, she adopts all those traditions and ceremonies, which were followed by her father Apu. She is modest and humble on account of this traditional upbringing. She is satisfied with her present condition and does not pine for what is not. She understands that the Memsahibs for whom, Apu and Ravi work, belong to a different class. She never appreciates displaying of female anatomy, which is shameless.

Presenting an ideal of good sister, she helps her sister Thangam in her need and gives new dresses to her daughters. When her husband Ravi condemns Thangam for the act of stealing by Puttanna, she opposes him raising her voice, "You blame her, what about him, stealing, taking what wasn't his is there no such thing as right and wrong. What's the matter with you that you can't see it" (*A Handful of Rice* 177).

She has sympathy for her sister but holds Puttanna responsible for stealing Apu's savings. She is not only a good sister but a goodmother also. She takes all troubles to give her children comfort and gets upset when Ravi beats Raju near the beach. She is shocked when her own son died of meningitis in the absence of timely medical assistance. Being a true daughter, she looks after Apu in his illness. She passes sleepless night for her father. She is like Cordelia nursing her father Lear when he is insane. Her sister Thangam is very Regan or Goneril who, after sucking her father's wealth, gives him up.

Hence, she is virtuous, blameless and possesses child-like innocence on her face. She plays well her traditional role of a good mother, an affectionate sister, an obedient and dutiful wife and a lovable daughter.

Quite contrary to Nalini who is a paragon of virtue like epical Sita, her sister Thangam betrays not only her father but also truth and honesty. She is an aberration of traditional image of woman-merely a stain on the fair sex. She is a selfish woman who with her husband Puttanna squanders Apu's wealth. It seems that she nags her husband for seeking a job but unfortunately tolerates and believes him when he says there is no job. She leaves her father in his illness and says nothing when her husband steals his hard earned money. Though she shows her unawareness to it, she keeps contact with her husband and finally goes to him with her children. Had she had a little sense of morality, she would not have done so. She is also equally responsible for the stealing episode. Yet, she simulates to be ignorant of it. She is mean, callous and incurable woman.

'A bitch,' 'a sow,' 'an old cow,' 'a many goat' are the terms used by Ravi for his mother-in-law Jayamma. She is the mother of a virtuous daughter like Nalini and also a mean one like Thangam. As the novel *A Handful of Rice* begins, she is shown as cruel, selfish and mean. She beats Ravi violently and chains him but hearing that he wants food, she feeds him. She is sympathetic, though she does not look so outwardly. She is a practical woman gifted with down to earth common sense. It is the result of her practical approach that she traps Puttanna and gives him Thangam in marriage. When she realizes that Ravi is mad in love with her daughter Nalini, she exploits him. She makes his income theirs and wishes to get rid of the burden of a daughter's marriage. She virtually manages the household affairs and skilfully solemnizes the marriage.

She is a greedy woman who looks both for money and sex. When Ravi beats Nalini, Jayamma is much concerned for her daughter, but when she realizes that there are no injuries, she thinks Apu had never once raised his hand to her. Her morality is at its low ebb. When Ravi asks her to forgive him for raping her, she retorts:

> What for last night? Do you think I care about that? Who cares what goes on between four walls? (*A Handful of Rice* 223)

But, she has a redeeming feature. With a strong sense of duty, she cares her husband in his illness, though without love. After his death, she honours her husband. "Perhaps I wronged him," said Jayamma, staring queerly at her daughter. "He was a good man your father, perhaps I did him wrong...but he was an old man you know, he seemed old to me even when married.... No matter, it is over" (*A Handful of Rice* 202).

Kamala Markandaya weans that in the process of change, all human values should not be last. *In The Coffer Dams*, she explores individual conflicts in the context of the opposition between tradition and modernity, responsibility and freedom and stresses the importance of sympathy in all human relationships through the protagonist Helen Clinton. She does a new experiment through Helen Clinton in bridging the gap between human values and industrial progress in the western style and in her endeavours; she thrives to a great extent. In doing so, she reminds us of Dr. Kenny who sympathizes with the poor villagers in *Nectar in a Sieve*. She is his female version and represents those healthy forces, which are active in the present day world to develop healthy human relations. Calling her, 'a novice in the East,' Elena J. Kalinnikova writes:

> Contrary to her husband, she finds in the natives not the rigid masks; but the ruthlessly exploited people who are in need of help. After learning the language of the tribal people, she establishes contact with the language of the tribal people; she establishes contact with the local

population. Humaneness is the bases of Helen's every act.... Her attitude is close to that of Kamala Markandaya who along with her character, shares the bitterness of insulted human dignity of the native inhabitants.[15]

Kamala Markandaya shows through her how the age of technology turns people into soulless mechanisms and kills human feelings in them. No doubt, striding cranes, excavators, bull dozers—all these dominate the builders of the dam, their thoughts and acts accelerating the speed of life but shortening the age of feelings. No wonder Clinton and Helen who are young couple in the beginning of the novel are translated into alienated beings as the story develops.

She feels kinship with the tribal people and is happier in their company than in that of memsahib like Millie Rawlings. When Clinton wonders how she can get along with natives, she tells him: "It's nothing to do with age. I just think of them as human beings that is all. You've got to get beyond their skies, darling. It's a bit of hurdle, but it is an essential one" (*The Coffer Dams*, 12). She is angry at the conduct of the Englishmen who, using the right of white people, have driven away the Indians from indigenous places, and have destroyed their huts and in their places have built for themselves comfortable bungalows. Her natural kindness makes her worry about the welfare of the tribal people. Like Dr. Kenny, she chides Bashiam for not protesting when the tribal people were forced to leave lands "without protest. Just got up and walked away, like animals" (*The Coffer Dams* 48).

Like Mira of *Some Inner Fury*, Helen Clinton thinks "These people aren't different class, they're like me, like people like me. What is for me, is for them, there's no other kind of yardstick that's worth anything" (*The Coffer Dams* 49).

She is in quest of harmony in an alien culture. She seeks and gets success in the development of relationship with the tribal chief, who adapts himself to make her comfortable in his country. She observes:

> The tribesmen...were changing. A backward people, whose primeval ways had exasperated successive

governments, monumental impediment in the path of progressive companies and administrations, even they had felt the glancing blow of social change. (*The Coffer Dams* 72)

She possesses human consideration and good will and becomes a symbol of love and fellow-feeling. She diverts her energy to the beneficiary activities for the tribal people in whom she recognizes the sense of community. She has a soft corner for Bashiam whom, the British and the Indian officer call 'Jungliwallah.' She makes him feel easy and comfortable in her company. When she finds him reeling in his uncertainty, she quickly reassures him with this ardent declaration.

Look at me, I've never been a memsahib. You're not some kind of freak to me. We're alike, we're freaks only to the caste. We come from not to each other. (*The Coffer Dams* 136)

Her prolonged visits disturb her husband who feels too much. He puts blames on the blasted country but she disagrees with him. Her relationship with Bashiam symbolizes perfection of kindred spirits. It is a union of minds rather than bodies, of cross-cultural human affinities rather than wanton sexuality. She has always been the centre of her husband's private life, "At the heart of his homecoming" (*The Coffer Dams* 142). Though there is gulf in their relationship, the quality of mutual respect which still exists, help in bridging the gulf. Her flexibility patches up the breach. Her progression to realization becomes intense and moving through her rebellious phase to an awareness of the total situation. She accepts her responsibility as Mrs. Helen Clinton.

In *The Nowhere Man*, Vasantha, wife of Srinivas, is purely a traditional woman who sticks to her Indian ways of living, dressing, eating and even dying, though transplanted on a foreign soil. She grows tired of moving like the gypsies and persuades her husband to own a house.

"There is no nomadic strain in us, that forces us to wander. Although it may well manifest in our children if we continue this vagabond existence." "...We will buy a house.

"We," she said, "my family, have for generations been accustomed to living in a house" (*The Nowhere Man* 17).

She makes plans for the future of her two sons—Seshu and Laxman. She has a bit of the British pragmatism despite her otherwise strong Indian character. But her practical sense leaves her, as it does not help when it is called for. She never thinks of herself as a Londoner. Indeed, she feels herself superior to the Whites in that she belongs to a religion of cosmic concepts. She describes Christianity which, in her opinion, is the religion for ten years old.

She builds castle in the air as she demarcates in the new house they have bought, areas for Laxman and Seshu, should they be married and have their own establishment. But, her son Laxman feels irritation at her sentimentality. She is proud of acquiring No. 5 Ashcrof Avenue, South London. "At last we have achieved something. A place of our own, where we can live according to our rights although in alien surroundings; and our children after us and after them theirs" (*The Nowhere Man* 21).

She is shocked at the death of her dear son Seshu who dies in harness. Her only surviving son Laxman throws cold water on her cherished dream of choosing a bride for him as he, after a meritorious war service, marries an English girl and settles down in Plymouth as a businessman. His living apart from her starts telling upon her too much. When even the birth of a child to Laxman does not help to unite the family, she collapses and dies leaving her husband all alone, desolate and depressed in the big mansion and the world.

Being a truly Indian, she feels a fish out of water in London and wishes to return to India. Indian blood bubbles in her veins. Though she is suffering from tuberculosis, she expresses her desire to return to her country. This shows she has patriotic feelings.

> When I am better, she said to her husband, we must return to our country. There is no reason, now that India is free, why we should not. Nor, she said painfully, is there anything, really to keep us here any more. (*The Nowhere Man* 38)

She is imbued with the spirit of Indian philosophy and becomes quite detached with the world in the evening of her life. Detachment grants peace and solace to her:

> She was very calm, very lucid, putting her affairs in order in so far as she could, though with a certain detachment, as if the concerns and liaisons of the world had fallen into peace, if not insignificance. Yet they were close; closer perhaps than many couples, since there had been no alternative vines and supports to which each might have attached.

> "It has been," said Vasantha hoarsely, the breath from her ruined lungs coming up rough, "a happy marriage." (*The Nowhere Man* 39)

She has been a devoted wife throughout her life. Her husband Srinivas, while throwing her ashes into the river, recalled the unforgettable moments, which he passed with her.

> ...he could not help feeling with Vasantha, who in her breath and bones had remained wholly Indian. She would have liked her remains committed to the currents of an Indian river, though she had scrupulously refrained from such onerous impositions; and now, watching her ashes drift away downstream. (*The Nowhere Man* 40)

The Western culture does not believe in throwing the ashes into pure water of the river. The policeman who represents this culture reacts when Srinivas throws her ashes. "The river's not the place for the rubbish." Srinivas takes it to his heart and replies pathetically:

> "It was not rubbish," said Srinivas, and found to his dismay that his throat was working painfully.
> "It was my wife." (*The Nowhere Man* 41)

Hence, she leaves an indelible imprint on the mind of Srinivas who, after her death, feels desolate and isolated in this world.

*Two Virgins* is about two village girls, the sisters Lalitha and Saroja, the elder running after a film director and coming to grief, and the younger (Saroja) moving from innocence to experience by living through the family's traumatic experience. The sisters are neatly contrasted, but while Lalitha's is the budget of experiences, it is Saroja's consciousness that observes, considers, weighs and places the developing events."[16]

Saroja, who is a thoroughly traditional, is the role model for the young girl. Apparently, she is not good-looking yet she possesses the beauty of soul. Lalitha's physical beauty gets eclipsed before her inner beauty. She has achieved a wonderful balance and stability partly under the influence of Aunt Alamelu and partly learning from her sister's experience. She is the ideal image of innocence and modesty.

She is never envious of her sister's beauty and smartness. She never suffers from any inferiority complex for not having magnetic personality like her sister. "Lalitha wishes her to become active, vivacious and smart like her. She is conscious of her weakness. Saroja knew she hadn't, she knew she was slow, she was often compared with Lalitha on the score and found wanting" (*Two Virgins* 77).

She is morally strong and presents an ideal of sister by consoling and stopping Lalitha from committing suicide.

> When Lalitha took the fork Saroja knew. It led to the well where the woman walked in her dripping needs, along the track where no one would walk by night. She fought the knowledge. She ran up panting and placed herself in her, she begged her to turn back, clung to her and brought her with the tears cascading down her face, but Lalitha would not. It's suicide. Well, said Saroja. (*Two Virgins* 182)

She learns much from her sister's bitter experiences, which leave an effective print of hatred for the city life on the mind of Saroja. Lalitha's tragic disillusionment with the ethics that dictate the pattern of living in the city serves as a practical lesson in growing up for her. She is quite satisfied with the life of her village and after experiencing the double standard of the life of the city, she wants to return to her village for, at home there were fields to rest her eyes on, "colour that changed with the seasons. The tender green of new crops, the tiny shades of harvest, the tints of freshly turned earth." She says further:

> You could have told the week and the month of the year by these alone. You know each grove, each acre, each homestead on it, who owned then and the names of the owners. You knew every pathway. No one could ever be lost, not by trying. The wells, the fields, each had its name; the well by the banyan, the field next to the mill. You always knew where you were. You knew who you were. The city took it all away from you. You were one in a hundred, in a thousand.... You might have been an amoeba. You drifted, amoeba-like. (*Two Virgins* 243)

She learns a lesson from Lalitha's bitter experience and comes back to the village with a firm determination to remain secure in her village without being misled by the attraction for the modern world. She has an adoration of life and a deep involvement with Nature and village life. Unlike ex-virgin Lalitha who opts tragically for the fate of the 'Town Mouse,' Saroja is satisfied with the life of the 'Country Mouse.' She is right in her suspicion that the males prowl through the streets "like wolves on the look out for girls" (*Two Virgins* 197). She confides absolutely in Chingleput, the sweet-seller. But, soon when she recognizes his evil design of her sexual exploitations, she rejects him.

> Saroja was not afraid, she knew too much, she had gone through too much to be afraid of anything. She knew she wasn't for him, she would never be. So, she drew away from him. (*Two Virgins* 250)

She saves herself from Devraj, the assistant of Mr. Gupta who attempts to make a pass at her. Joseph compares her with Miriam Henderson and writes: "Saroja's is a stream of thought, Miriam's is stream of consciousness."[17]

In *The Golden Honeycomb*, Kamala Markandaya's audacious enterprise is to introduce with an authentic touch of national awakening leading to mass struggle against the cruel British rulers. This bold attempt is successful because of its skilful handling of the characters of the British and the Indians. More importance is given to men than women in a historical novel. It is only partially true in case of *The Golden Honeycomb*. Characters like Manjula, Mohini and Usha have their roots in Indian traditions. Manjula and Mohini play pivotal role in the affirmation of the continuity of the essential cultural values amid the manifold political changes in modern India. They are the model of India's traditional womanhood in guiding, re-guiding, shaping and re-shaping the fate of Bawajiraj III and Rabindranath. What they are, they are made by Manjula and Mohini who fire enthusiasm and inspiration in them. Following the path shown by these women characters, Rabi provides peace and progress to the people of the state.

Manjula opposes the British rule not openly but secretly as she advises Mohini, not to marry but to live freely from the clutches of the British so that she may have got opportunity to make Rabi red-hot iron ready for struggle by imbibing the Indian culture in him. She enlightens her grandson Rabi at time and fuses into him anti-British feelings. She is quite anxious about the future heir to the gaddi. She favours Rabi, the Pandit and the Dewan.

Mohini is the woman who injects patriotism not only in the veins of her lover Bawajiraj but also in the veins of her son Rabi. For her, the British are the civilized wolves (*The Golden Honeycomb* 405). She does not like Bawajiraj's unshrinking loyalty towards the British ruler. She usually calls Sir Arthur not Sir Arthur but as Bania Sahib. She lets her paramour know about the exploitations of the Britishers who, in her opinion, are here for their financial and territorial gains and that they are least interested in the uplift of the Indian people.

In *Pleasure City*, Kamala Markandaya has not done justice to her women characters. No significant roles are for women as she has concentrated her whole attention on men—Rikki and Tully. It seems that in *Pleasure City*, pleasure, though in possession of women, is meant for men. To give a symbolical meaning to Rikki-Tully relationship, she has sketched them artistically. To paint them in bright colours, she has taken the colour of her women's share. She enters the male world but forgets the password to exit. Her mind is charged with male fire but a female river is flowing in her heart. No sooner does this fire extinguish than she is conscious of the female river and gives it place for its flowing. In her still mood, she breathes life into her female world and makes her women alive. Mrs. Bridie, Amma, Valli, Corinna, Zevera, Mrs. Contractor, Mrs. Pearl, Mrs. Chari, Mrs. Lockwood, Mrs. Lovat etc., arise, move, feel, understand and contribute a lot in making the threads of Tully-Rikki relationship stronger.

*Pleasure City* marks the 'voyage in' and celebrates the essential superiority of Indian culture and values over the western...with the emergence of a regime of essentialization—Africanizing the Africans, orientalizing the oriental, westernizing the western—in the post-colonial era, Markandaya's text assumes greater relevance as one that cuts across boundaries and suggests the possibilities of relationship across frontiers.[18] And her women characters especially western—Mrs. Bridie, Corrina, Mrs. Pearl etc. strengthen the possibilities of relationship.

Mrs. Bridie, an angel in human body, has come in this world to help the poor and needy and to relieve them of their sufferings. Her first real neophyte is Rikki whom she moulds into such cast as she wishes. She draws the child Rikki onto her lap and reads to him out of the Bible. She always thinks of the fishermen and their children. Like Dr. Kenny, she is sympathetic to all. She runs her school for their children in one shuttered room of her tumble down house. She sees something new in Rikki and starts taking interest in him. She notices that he is regular and reads English lessons with keen interest. Rikki portrays her beautifully:

> ...tall, bony woman with her yellowing skin and her tired eyes, who looked so different from everyone around.... He thought about her bosom. So flat, he could feel through the stuff of her dress, not at all like the full globes of her mother. He thought it must be so from never having brimmed with milk for children. (*Pleasure City* 6)

As she is childless, she pours her motherly affection on Rikki. She is, Rikki thinks, such a woman as possesses "the key to locked, mysterious boxes that he barely knew existed except for the barest outlines that were showing up hazily in the distance" (*Pleasure City* 6)

She takes it to her heart when Muthu comes to take him away from school, as it is prawn-fishing season. She believes 'Food is not everything in life.' She feels pain of others. She takes away pen from Rikki's hand when she sees his palms galled and says: "Your hands will have to heal before you do 'any more writing." (*Pleasure City* 12). But, when he asks for pen as he can manage, she advises him: "If a thing is worth, it is worth doing well. You must always aim to be immaculate." (*Pleasure City*16). She takes care of him well and pours her heart's feelings. She stares him again and again as she sees the image of her son if she had one. She asks:

"He would have been like you, you know Rikki."

'Who?' He could hardly guess whom she meant.

"If I had had a son; she replied looking him full in the face." (*Pleasure City* 16)

After such blissful conversation, she breathes her last.

That—yellow stick—of—a—woman! (*Pleasure City* 341) is always present on the screen of Rikki's mind. Even after her death, she is alive in his memory. He takes guidance from time to time remembering her valuable saying. At the end of the novel, he repeats the words of Mrs. Bridie: "There was a time and a season, for everything. A time to sow and a time to reap" (*Pleasure City* 341). In spite of her infertility, she is fertile as she considers others children as her own. She presents the image of mother—Universal Mother.

Amma in her traditional role presents herself as a mother who makes no difference between the real son and foster one. She takes the responsibility of Rikki's bringing up as she thinks that the poor one has none in the world after his parents' death. She showers her motherly love making him feel easier and more comfortable. "Call me Amma, if you like, she said, busy with the bellows and charcoal so as not it embarrass the child. I am your mother now, and lucky to be" (*Pleasure City* 9). She looks after him well and makes him eat more and more so that he may become strong and master the sea. She takes care of his health. "Eat," she urged. "Eat and grow up big and strong, so that you can master the sea" (*Pleasure City* 18).

In spite of her traditional role, she is curious to know more and more but is not anxious of the future as Rukmani is in *Nectar in a Sieve*. She is rejoiced at the sight of Shalimar, which looks beautiful to her. She goes in its building and is lost. To press switch in Shalimar, is a new experience.

Mrs. Pearl, as the name suggests, is indeed, a precious pearl. The dust of materialism is on this pearl. Indian spiritualism with its brush cleans it, with its fire, purifies it and with its spray, polishes it. Rikki describes Mrs. Pearl, a new arrival at Shalimar:

> Gray curls with blue lights in them, a dumpy figure not improved by the flowered costume—a glance and he had placed her firmly in the brigade of aged and authoritative ladies that overflowed the camp. (*Pleasure City* 137)

She has an inclination towards spiritualism. She loves water and wishes to stay in it forever. She is desirous of learning swimming but thinks herself a hopeless case. Water symbolizes re-birth—death of materialism. She feels she is too late to learn. "I'm a hopeless case I know, but I've always wanted to be able" (*Pleasure City* 139). Rikki sympathizes with her and tries to understand the feelings of this lonely woman. She gives him money but he returns it. She advises him to take it as he has given his time and hence, he should get its compensation. She asks him: Why not Rikki? Time; she blunted, is money. She did not think it was. Time was mysterious stuff, not an issue from a human mint.

She takes interest in helping others by showing sympathy or giving money. When Rikki refuses to take her money, she feels too much. She asks him. "Is my money polluted, or something?" (*Pleasure City* 141). She is sympathetic and kind to the orphan. She tells him: "So am I sure; she said, and rose above the fumes to even higher reaches of honesty and self-knowledge. I'm old. I'm rich. I'm alone in the world except for one niece by marriage. It pleases me to give. Why can't you take?" (*Pleasure City* 142).

During her visit to the cave, she finds a child there, takes it and looks after it. She nurses the infant developing an attachment. She finds the country is growing on her. "She also discerned—perhaps insights followed, inevitably—she was not alone" (*Pleasure City* 212). The infant is named 'Kali' to invoke the protection of the powerful goddess. "Where she is, she's looked after" (*Pleasure City* 214). She loves Kali and pours her heart to the infant.

> "And who knows", said Mrs. Pearl now and then, to Kali, or anyone else within hearing. "One of these days I might even carry you off to England with me." And rocked and tickled the child under the chin lovingly, only half playing with the lovely, crazy notion. (*Pleasure City* 215)

She loves Zavera but her parties weary her. She wishes to go to those places that prove solace to her soul. She wishes to commune with nature. She is a tranquil woman who is never tired of waiting. She has given up wearing shoes—another step on the route to her nirvana. She finds herself wrong in the description when she compares Shalimar with Avalon. Praising Avalon, she says:

> Neither love, nor hate went into its fabric. Meticulously built for selling itself, it fulfilled that purpose. Shalimar went whoring after money.... Shalimar did nothing of the sort. Its wiles were more courtly, those of a courtesan. (*Pleasure City* 332)

Her preference for Avalon to Shalimar shows her inclination towards spiritualism and not towards materialism.

Kamala Markandaya's women are caught in the whirlpool of tradition. They face a heroic struggle to come out but fail as the chain of tradition binds their feet. They muster up and with great force; some of them break it but not completely, come out and enter the domain of 'New Woman'. They still retain traditional colour though faint in the dazzling light of this new domain. The changes in time bring changes in the circle of their activities and they adapt themselves to new environment but their basic traditional mental vision remains unchanged.

All the women characters feel the warmth of changes, struggle in their minds whether they should reject the old ones and welcome the new ones, find out a possible solution out of these inner dialogues in following the via media and ultimately vote for transformation re-evaluating and re-defining the concepts in the new light of changes. They are in the train of modernity and in this wonderful journey they get experiences learn a lot, see the world from its windows but never pull away their roots from the soil that is tradition.

Kamala Markandaya's women like *Rukmani* who fights a heroic battle against unfavourable circumstances of her life to keep her family united, *Mira* who sacrifices her love for the country, *Premala* who does her best to adjust in the modern world of her husband but, ultimately, gets peace in social service and dies for the noble cause, *Sarojini,* who believes in the faith-healer, becomes ready for operation to save the family, *Anasuya* who makes Caroline realize of the Indian culture and traditions, *Nalini* who, like a true wife, guides her husband Ravi at every step, *Saroja* who controls her passions, keeps balance and remains virgin, *Vasantha* who supports her husband morally and psychologically, *Helen Clinton* who beacons to the tribal people out of darkness, *Manjula* and Mohini who instill patriotic feelings in Rabindranath and make him ready for the final battle against the British, *Mrs. Pearl* who believes in Indian spiritualism, *Amma* who makes no difference between her own son and foster one and *Mrs. Bridie* who presents an ideal of Universal Mother—are exemplary traditional bricks that build the traditional image of woman. But, under the garb of tradition, they have the latent material of modernity, less in quantity though weighty in quality.

## Notes and References

1. "The Princess", Poems by Alfred Lord Tennyson, ed., M. Bozman Vol. 1, 245.

2. "Gender Relation" *Indian Society* (N.B.T., India, 1990), 112.

3. "On The Construction of Gender: Hindu Girls in Patrilineal India." Karuna Channa, ed. *Socialization, Education and Women*. Delhi: Orient Longman, 1988, 175.

4. Rao, A.V. Krishna, *The Indo-Anglian Novel and The Changing Tradition*. Mysore: Rao and Raghvan, 1972, 57.

5. *Image of Woman in The Indo-Anglian Novel* (New Delhi: Sterling Publishers, 1979), 51.

6. K.R.S. Iyengar, *Indian Writing in English*, 438.

7. *Indo-Anglian Literature 1800-1970: A Survey* (Madras: Orient Longman, 1976) 85.

8. K.R.S. Iyengar: *Indian Writing in English*, 440.

9. Ed. S.K. Desai, Experimentation with Language. *An Indian Writing in English* (Fiction, Kolhapur: Shivaji University, 1974), 130.

10 "Anatomy of Silence in A Silence of Desire" *Indian Women Novelists* Set II, Vol. II ed. by R.K. Dhawan, Prestige Books, N. Delhi. 238.

11. K.R.S. Iyengar, *Indian Writing in English*, 444-45.

12. K.R.S. Iyengar, *Indian Writing in English*, 446-47.

13. "Continuity and Change in the Novels of Kamala Markandaya" *Perspective on Kamala Markandaya*, 14.

14. "Markandaya's A Handful of Rice: A Study A Dreamy Youth" *Six Indian Novelists in English*, 164.

15. "The Hindu Woman From London: Kamala Markandaya." *Indian-English Literature: A Perspective*, 161.

16. K.R.S. Iyengar, *Indian Writing in English*, 741-42.

17. Margaret P. Joseph, *Kamala Markandaya*, 144.

18. "The Discourse of Resistance: A Reading of Kamala Markandaya's Pleasure City," Dr. D. Maya, *Indian Writing in English* Vol. 3, ed. by Bhatnagar, 113.

# Person: New Woman in the Making

## 4

"When I heard someone remarks 'We never allow our daughter to go out' or 'I can't do that, my husband would not like it,' it sounded a very peculiar, alien jargon. As if I thought, women were property, not persons." Quoting this famous statement of Nayantara Sahgal, Seema Suneel writes:

> This awakening among the feminists and women writers has helped them to project in their writing the image of new woman. In such times, when radical change is going on all over the country, it has become quite desirable for woman to redefine her new role and determine the parameters so as to become an integral part of family and society, striking a true balance between extreme feminism and the conventional role of subjugation and self-denial.[1]

It is clear from Seema Suneel's views that extreme feminism is not of practical value, nor the conventional role of subjugation and self-denial is praise-worthy. A balance is required to maintain the purity of relations and hence, a new face of the woman has emerged in Indian English fiction. But, it does not mean that the new woman is merely an aggregate of certain personality traits to be studied through the methodology of social sciences. She is a being in her own way and is on the process of becoming. Though it is difficult to define the New Woman, she can be defined as woman who seeks self-fulfilment through self-expression in a milieu where there is mutuality, understanding and affection. Sharad Srivastava writes in this connection:

The woman is 'new' when she analysis and reflects upon her position essentially as a woman in the scheme of things which includes the social, moral and spiritual fields.[2]

A new woman is completely different from the woman who thinks of seeking equality with men, asserting her own personality and emphasizing on her own rights as a woman. She is gifted with depth and rationale thinking and is aware of value system. Quite contrary to the new woman is the woman whose pet words are self-assertion and dominance and who calls herself emancipated and economically independent. Such face of the woman is diagnosed as aberration. Thus, the new woman, clinging to her basic values modifying herself according to the modifying circumstances, goes ahead on the way seeking for her own identity with new depth and getting recognition but never like the aberration type. Sharad Srivastava writes:

> Like the traditional woman, the new woman, too, tolerates, makes adjustments for the family and the husband, understands him and even forgives him but nowhere do we find her changing or moulding her basic personality.[3]

There is something distinct in the women characters of Kamala Markandaya—something in their spiritual and emotional make up that express itself in their attitude to persons and events. In these women characters, there is a deep longing for self-fulfilment through self-expression. Kamala Markandaya has realistically presented emotional, moral and spiritual problems of the new woman. The new woman in her novels is not in 'proper' but in 'making.' But, her women characters are able to project the image of the new woman as 'person.' Usha in *The Golden Honeycomb* emerges with her feminist cry "Whoever heard of a revolution for man only? No, it's everyone. Men and women. They do belong to the same species."

The women characters of her novels, though not conscious, though not fully aware, yet are concerned with the fundamental question—the lot of women. They analyze this through the metaphors that deal with the themes of suffering, dominance, urge for companionship, etc. It is through these metaphors that the moral and spiritual needs of the new woman are projected. According to Krishnaswamy, in Kamala Markandaya's novels, "the quest for autonomy leads her to nurturance of warm familial relationship, which in turn progresses towards imaginative sympathy for the human race."[4]

The credit goes to Rukmani, the protagonist in *Nectar in a Sieve* for holding the flag of new woman. She has achieved success in realizing her goal while following the norms and values, which the society has laid down. She is not a rebel but likes to follow the via media. In spite of the blasts of misfortunes, she has survived and has discovered an identity. She has shown that there is no need to rebel against the society if one wishes to have a place and make others realize of one's presence and identity. She knows well that one can't escape the world. Her pet words are: live sincerely, think seriously and do not break the norms and values of the society. One can achieve one's identity living in the society, not out of society. She makes others especially male characters feel of her importance. She is endowed with an awareness of the possibilities of life. She sees value in living. For her, the act of living is important. Praising Rukmani, G.R. Taneja observes:

> Young Rukmani's reactions to the world around her are motivated by a recognition that life is for living and when going gets tough human mind must draw its strength from an unambiguous acceptance of the inescapable and that admit the desire to escape is anathema. Not to break-up or destroy, but to persist and rebuild is what life is about. Not self-pity but self-esteem is what human existence must derive its sustenance from.[5]

She is a woman not to be confined to home. She comes out of her home to lighten the burden of her husband by working in the field. She is the image of new woman who learns how to read and write and teaches her children. In the city, when she is facing adverse circumstances, she tries to earn something to keep body and soul together. The venture is not very successful, but it speaks volumes of her courage, determination and far-sightedness. She faces the twin whips of tradition and modernity. She can neither say good-bye to tradition nor accepts modernity thoroughly. She is intelligent enough to choose the via media and in doing so, she becomes the child of transition. Uma Parameswaran thinks that Rukmani is a child of the transition between the insular, autonomous village life of old and the new village dependent upon urban civilization and in constant contact with it. She faces life and shows her maturity in responding to its changing hues. By using reason and intellect in life, she has become exemplary character. Life is meant to live. Live hopefully is the mantra that she gives and "that by being a Karam-yogi, one could live even without nectar—the fruit of action."[6]

Irawaddy or Ira as she is lovingly called, is the first child of Nathan and Rukmani. She is fair child, lovely and dimpled with soft gleaming hair. Her physical charms are wall-matched with the nobility and beauty of her soul. Through her life-story, Kamala Markandaya has depicted the grim and shocking picture of the degradation and corruption that hunger brings in. She is married at the age of fourteen accepting silently the choice of her parents. Being a victim of fate and human monstrosity, she is brought back to her mother's house by her husband because she is proved as barren. She knows well that she will have to pass the rest of her life as a deserted wife in the home of her parents. Later on, she is cured of her barrenness but by that time, her husband has taken another woman, and so cannot take her back. She does not complain or revolt, but accepts her lot for it was to be.

She sells her body to feed her starving brother and to save him from death. It is not an immoral act but an act of supreme self-sacrifice like that of Tess in Hardy's *Tess of the D'urbervilles*. She is glad to sacrifice it for, by doing so, she can ameliorate the suffering of the sick and dying Kuti, and contribute her mite to her destitute family. Her father Nathan is wrong in considering the money she brings to be sinful, it is not sinful, it is the result of noble and heroic self-sacrifice, which sanctifies and purifies it. This supreme self-sacrifice ennobles her and imparts a heroic grandeur to her.

It is in one of the encounters with men that she conceives a baby whom she accepts with a sense of resignation. This child is a sickly Albino, different from the other children and so more an object of contempt than pity. However, she is a devoted mother who nurses the child affectionately, is proud of him, as any mother of a normal child would be, and endures patiently the shame and humiliation that is heaped upon her for his being, a 'bastard.' She suffers terribly but she suffers silently without ever giving an idea of her deep spiritual anguish.

Kamala Markandaya has made her bold enough to declare that she will not let her brother die from starvation. When her father scolds her severely "I will not have you parading at night," she replies to him in an equally determining tone, "Tonight and tomorrow and every night, so long as there is need. I will not hunger any more" (*Nectar in a Sieve* 103). The new woman arises in her as she thinks of saving her brother even at cost of bearing the name of harlot. Unlike Kunthi, she sells her body and becomes like Shankar by drinking the poison (prostitution) to give life to her brother. As she has learnt never to yield, she musters up courage and defies the society by giving birth to a child. She nurses it like a devoted mother. G.R. Taneja has tried to analyze the question of woman's search for identity. He says: "…meaning, alienation, or fulfilment in marriage within and without, must be part of the larger question of life and living."[7] Ira proves that she can live and search her own identity. Believing in life for living, she defines and sets her own parameters of life without considering the dual code of morality of the society.

Kamala Markandaya's *Some Inner Fury* is full of fire on account of some inner fury of three women characters—Mira, the narrator, Roshan, the firebrand freedom fighter and Premala, a complete housewife. These women characters are pilgrims in their own way as they are on a journey seeking answers to their questions on the meaning of life. In search of their self-hood, they step out of their houses with some doubts in their mind and place their feet on the different paths where armies of troubles are waiting for them. The paths differ but the goal is the same.

Mirabai, who is provided the western aroma, makes up her mind to marry Richard with or without her mother's approval. She thinks she is the mistress of her own life and has freedom to take decision concerning her life. Her mother asks her to wait when she makes her know of her decision of marrying Richard but never wishes to leave her love unfulfilled. She moves in with her lover Richard and crosses the first threshold towards freedom from tradition and cultural stigmas. Though she crosses it, she has her doubts:

> Words which anyone might say to anyone, warned my wary suspicious self, instantly raising its guard against possible hurt, a formality, a courtesy, a manner of speaking, no more, but my other self, warm impetuous, unafraid, cried that these words for me meant more, much more—And I, the arbiter, placing the truth half-way between, found, even so, that the glow was not doused. (*Some Inner Fury*, 91)

No sooner does she meet Roshan than she comes to like her and decides to work for her paper. She learns how to make the society feel of her identity. While living in the company of Roshan who "would not give up being free like that for anything," (*Some Inner Fury* 189) she finds it quite incommunicable to make the old generation understand that the self-hood can be achieved if one is free in one's orbit.

> It was more an instinctive understanding than a reasoned one: if anyone had asked me for an explanation. I should have been hard put to it supply a coherent one. But then none who belonged to my generation would have needed to do so, and to those who did not belong the sense and the spirit would alike have been incommunicable. It is this shared understanding, this common awareness, diffuse in the atmosphere, yet not absorbed by all, which makes the ground split, the crevasse to appear, between one generation and the next. (*Some Inner Fury* 189)

She meets Richard at the Government House unexpectedly and the cold fire gets the gust and the flames of love start enkindling in their hearts to the height of maturing true love. She analyses life, becomes serious and is lost in thinking.

> And it was our life, by our own choice, by being born when we were, even, if one were so minded by destiny. We created it, as much as it created us; belonged to it as much.... To keep our peace we would have to go back then to the world from which we come, to which we would always return because it was a part of us even as the earth was of these others who stayed, we could no more renounce it than a bird the air, or fish the sea, or any other creature its element.... (*Some Inner Fury* 192)

She takes a bold step as she goes with her lover on a holiday tour. She believes in love and favours love over marriage. She sets the model of love without marriage, not of marriage without love, as is the case of Kit and Premala. She gives herself to her love with full devotion. She wishes:

"...we could be together all the time."

"We shall be soon."

"But you may have to go away."

"I'll come back—I'll always come back to you!" (*Some Inner Fury* 199)

This is the true love that both of them develop for each other. Love, which is a substitute for marriage here, becomes, "a talisman that would somehow keep us together, protecting us against war, the world, everything" (*Some Inner Fury* 199). She bleeds inwardly, but silently suffers for the sake of the country. She is not selfish and knows that love always gives, never takes. Love is the unconditional sacrifice for her. What though she is not married! Her love is great, high and far above marriage. It is the marriage of two minds, two souls not physically but mentally and spiritually. By her sacrifice, she never wishes to show her greatness to the unsentimental world.

It is all one.... In a hundred years, it is all one; and still my heart wept tearless, desolate silently to itself. But what matter to universe, I said to myself, if now and then a world is born or a star should die, or what matter to the world, if here and there a man should fall or a head should break. (*Some Inner Fury* 286)

In Roshan, Kamala Markandaya portrays the liberated woman of modern India. Having been educated in England and on the Western values, she has a dual citizenship and feels quite at home in both the worlds.

Born in one world, educated in another, she entered both and moved in both with ease and nonchalance. It was a dual citizenship, which few people had, which a few may have spurned, but many more envied, and which she herself simply took for granted. And curiously enough, both worlds were glad to welcome her in their midst. (*Some Inner Fury* 142-43)

She appears in the novel for the first time at Kit's wedding "in a chiffon sari coloured like a rainbow, and slippers with rhinestone heels, and a mouth as bright and vivid as a geranium petal—who was easily the most striking" (*Some Inner Fury* 68). She is at home in whatever situation she finds herself. She attracts attention in the prison with the "cheapest of homespun saris (*Some Inner Fury* 69). She is frank, educated, talented and motivated towards an inspiring goal—that of winning freedom for her country in an enlightened way. She is a born leader and always, "wherever she was and in whatever company, Roshan was always the one who arrested attention" (*Some Inner Fury* 69).

Roshan is pleasing and talks cheerfully. Kit introduces her saying that "she used to write poetry then. I don't know what she does now—something outrageous, I expect." At this Roshan replies wittingly, "I used to call myself a poet," No one else did, so I had to give up. I'm a columnist now" (*Some Inner Fury* 69). Bubbling up with vitality and free spirit, she has only one object in her life and that is to fulfil her personality in her own way and for this no stake is too dear for her. In her pursuit of freedom, Roshan, the rebel, breaks the bonds of marriage. "My husband and I have parted company," Roshan said, "I didn't want to shock her it would have, wouldn't it?" (*Some Inner Fury* 70). It is perhaps this show of consideration that, in spite of her separation from her husband, "We haven't lived together for years," she said, "We used to squabble like anything when we did, but now—funny thing—we're the best of friend" (*Some Inner Fury* 70).

Though she has sympathy for the west and is on the intimate terms with individual westerners, she is truly Indian at heart and takes active part in the political struggle against Britain. When she is released after serving a term of imprisonment, Mira's asking, if she was sorry for her life in prison, she remarks confidently:

> What do you think? Of course I'm not sorry! I'd rather go to the devil my own way than be led to heaven by anyone else. And I wouldn't give up being free like that for anything...it hasn't always been that way—No, not even for me! (*Some Inner Fury* 189)

Her 'forwardness' may not always find favour with the older generation but even though she may break any norms, she can understand that others may want to follow them. In her search for freedom, she does not bind others in any way because each one has to grapple with circumstances, and find one's own via media to arrive at a definition of self. So when Govind is staying with her, she asks Mira also to stay with her not because she cares but because Govind does—"They know what I did was for the cause, but if Govind really stays with me it'll provide a scandal unless I can point to a chaperone" (*Some Inner Fury* 172).

She does not believe in using violent means for the freedom movement. When Govind, another rebel character who belongs to the terrorist, approaches her for help, she replies:

> Everybody is interested in freedom...only, we do not all agree on the means to the end, as I think you know too. (*Some Inner Fury* 126)

She believes that "There is no power in violence...only destruction" (*Some Inner Fury* 126). Ultimately, looking at him steadily, she says, "I am not really interested in destruction." (*Some Inner Fury* 126). However, she helps Govind when he is imprisoned for subversive activities. She not only pays the fees but also provides an alibi for him. "She testified for him at the last minute...swore he'd spent the night with her.... It was cleverly done" (*Some Inner Fury* 172).

She exemplifies the eternal woman who has to assert her inner being and bear the consequence of doing so. She attempts to create a space herself in which she can strengthen her being and claim that which is lost with dignity. She represents the symbol of the woman's psyche, which considers woman to be helpless and dependent. She becomes a role-model for Premala and Mira and shows them the spirit of freedom with a flaming torch. Mira is impressed by her and considers her to be the pathfinder.

> She gave me the chance to go and I took it; and though I left my home. I discovered at least the gateway to the freedoms of the mind and gazed entranced upon the vista of endless extensions of which the spirit is capable. (*Some Inner Fury* 71)

Roshan possesses a strong stamina for the advocacy of the New Woman and is a symbol of the resurgence of Indian women in the wake of the National Movement. She resembles Rajeshwari (of K.S. Venkataramani's *Kandan, the Patriot*) who renounces the comforts of her luxurious life to dedicate herself to the cause of India's struggle for independence.

Premala in *Some Inner Fury* is a misfit in the world of Kitsmay and, hence, fails miserably. She grows lonely without an outlet for her pent-up affections. Her wifehood remains incomplete in absence of a child. She brings up an orphan girl without caring her husband's disapproval of it. She rebels and the bringing up of the orphan girl is the first act to make her husband realize that she is not mere property or possession at his disposal but a woman who has her own identity. She enjoys many a pleasure of unfulfilled motherhood in the possession of the orphan girl. This unsatisfactory marriage also makes her a social worker. The saying that 'broken hearted women are often driven to become good reformers' is quite true in her case. She becomes busy in her social work, as she needs an outlet. If her husband had really loved and accepted her as she was without forcing her persona into rigid moulds, the question of her becoming a reformer would not have arisen.

Govind is the only man who reads the closed book of her heart. He touches the chord of her heart but her traditional twist will not allow her to accept him to be her lover. She has fire but this fire cools off as soon as she realizes herself and sublimates her feelings. She puts up a heroic struggle between her instinctual individual urge and the demands of the group. She votes for the group making her busy in its social work. Her preference to serve the group makes her a person or new woman and this step of hers symbolizes the step of the Indian woman towards liberation.

Speech is silver, silence is gold but, silence, sometimes, is responsible for misunderstanding and creating gulf in relations. Though Sarojini (*A Silence of Desire*) has done nothing wrong, Dandekar doubts her chastity and calls her a 'soiled woman'. She takes it to her heart and opposes her husband's spying on her:

'So you watched me'

'Yes. And if I had watched you sooner, it would have been better for us, all of us, because a soiled woman is no good to anyone, not even to her children, do you understand that? (*A Silence of Desire* 71)

A new woman awakens in her when her husband doubts her. She says, "You listened to the office gossip and you spied on me" (*A Silence of Desire* 72). She opposes him and says boldly: "But you have eyes. If you wish to see you can. See for yourself—there is nothing to stop you" (*A Silence of Desire* 73). She is deeply hurt and is exasperated at the suspicious behaviour of Dandekar who has doubted her moral rectitude, her chastity, the preservation of her marriage vows.

Her husband feels the ground slipping away under his feet when he comes to know that she goes to the Swamy for the cure of her growth. He becomes a statue-like but speaks with difficulty: "Is he—a faith healer?" She replies boldly and unhesitatingly:

> Yes, you can call it healing by faith, or healing by the grace of God, if you understand what that means. But I do not expect you to understand—you with your western notions, your superior talk of ignorance and superstition when all it means is that you don't know what lies beyond reason and you prefer not to find out.... And none is a disease to be cured and so you would have sent me to hospital and I would have died there. (*A Silence of Desire* 87-88)

But, a question arises here why Sarojini cannot trust her husband in such minor thing, after such a long period of marriage. Marriage is a sacred bond based on mutual trust. If she cannot trust her husband, she has no right to expect his. It is here that Kamala Markandaya makes her commonplace because she fails to keep the fundamental thing on which marriage is based, and that is mutual trust. However, she accuses Dandekar for this very reason. It seems she adopts the policy that offence is the best defence. But, this offence becomes the cause of distrust. Sometimes, too much love creates suspicion. She does not wish to lose her love and, hence, feels safe in not taking her husband into confidence about the faith healer. Yet, silence is more responsible in creating doubts and, at this stage, speech is to be desired, when speech comes to the fore, all doubts and suspicions disappear. Ultimately, mutual trust is restored.

Annabel in *Possession* represents the liberated and uninhibited English girls of the fifties. She is a rebel, a girl who had turned down her family's traditional plans for organized displays in the marriage market. The novelist depicts her personality saying: "Annabel, a girl of eighteen, is small, slim, ordinary-looking: bright brown eyes, brownish-gold hair cut in ragged unchin style, the short spiky ends appearing all over her head" (*Possession* 189).

The freshness of eighteen years is on her face and it looks more and more when she speaks or laughs or argues or disagrees. She is frank and leads a free life. She develops a liaison with Val and hopes to marry him. Kamala Markandaya describes Val and Annabel in a party.

"Perfumes of Araby," he sang absurdly, poising a crisp over Annabel.

"Open, Annabel!" she resisted, laughing, pink mouth closing over small white teeth, and suddenly she was provocative, their exchanges were alive with sexual undertones, what had been banter was love-play, an enactment of the cycle of pursuit, retreat, capture, surrender, given in shadow-play and mime" (*Possession* 190-91).

Annabel, for Val is beautiful—without shame and innocent. Anasuya makes him aware of Caroline Bell who will never favour them. And, it happens so; they find a big obstruction from Caroline on their way. But, she is quite happy as she realizes that Val loves her and this is her trump card.

Caroline is not in favour of the friendship that is developing between Val and Annabel. She does succeed in separating them by creating such circumstances that Annabel breaks up her relation with him. Though "liberated soul," she looks the world of her love through the spectacles of Caroline who shows Annabel what she wishes to show. She forgets the love and purity that lie in it. She is poor as she fails to understand Caroline's real motive believing in what she says: "Emotional," "Unstable." Foreigners are. Dear Annabel, you must realize they aren't like us...you would never be able to rely on one of them" (*Possession* 206). And, so, she bids goodbye to Val for good under Caroline's impression.

Nalini in *A Handful of Rice* is the only sheet anchor of Ravi's life. She shows him the light on the dark path, which he has opted. She is quite satisfied with what she has. She realizes the conditions and circumstances and makes him dispel his romantic notions. No doubt, she is traditional but a new woman emerges in her when she takes out her husband from the mud of amoral world. She attracts him from his erratic movements to her own self, checks his wild flights of imagination and thus with the passage of time, becomes the voice of realism and sanity. When he promises her a soft bed, she says, "Such ideas. Do you think we are grand people? Is not this good enough for us?" (*A Handful of Rice* 77). She says, "I'm happy." When he returns home late at night, she gets angry and is not able to tolerate others' comments on her husband. She says: "I just don't want to hear them calling you vagabond again, that's all" (*A Handful of Rice* 77). She adjusts with her husband bearing beating and abuses. But when her tolerance exhausts, she goes out of the house and returns only at his repeated requests. She tells Kumaran: "I try and try. I swear to you. I try but it makes no difference. He is angry with me. All the time I don't why. I can't bear it any more?" (*A Handful of Rice* 224).

Nalini is emotionally mature. She understands the world and does not feel it like an infant as Ravi does. She has none of Ravi's foolish cravings. She knows that ordinary person like her can never be like them. She lives not in the dream world but in the world of reality and makes Ravi realize of it.

Helen Clinton represents the new generation of sensitive and sensible English women in *The Coffer Dams*. She is vibrant and puissant lady who believes in enlarging the scope of human relationship through understanding. She gets satisfaction in building bridges of understanding while her husband gets satisfaction in constructing the coffer dams. She perceives that the vastness of the tradition sustains tribal people. She takes the natives in her confidence and searches new realm of social interaction that aggrandizes her cultural consciousness. She reacts with ease: "Delighted her too, opened up a new acceptances, filled a want that was in her quiescent but ready to flare something in England had starved her" (*The Coffer Dams* 42).

She has a thirst for the fullness of life, which is always related to the cultural context. She seeks a life in which qualities of satisfaction and excellence are present. She realizes that machines make people inhumane and deprive them of feeling. Head kills heart. Materialism kills spiritualism. She retrogrades from her husband Clinton farther and farther each day because he sees himself only as 'builder.' For him, concrete and steel are more important than human beings. She feels no hesitation in scolding her husband Clinton for showing cruelty to the tribal people. She flares up at his indifference to human feelings. She is dead against his indifference towards the tribal people. She says: "Don't human beings matter anything to you? Do they have to be a special kind of flesh before they do?" (*The Coffer Dams* 105).

She is bold enough to put mirror before Clinton so that he may see his real face. She feels no hesitation in calling a spade a spade. She hates him for following dual policy in the treatment of the tribal people. He does not prevent Bashiam intentionally from operating defective crane. The consequence is that Bashiam becomes a crippled. Iyengar says, "She survives the shock and charges her husband pointedly. He (Bashiam) was not told, and could not know since it was a concealed defect (in the crane). Had Clinton, out of jealousy, deliberately laid the trap? Had Bashiam, out of a vague sense of guilt, half-deliberately walked into the trap?"[8]

She does not believe in man-made gulf of caste, colour and culture. She knows only one religion—religion of humanity based on love and fellow feeling and follows it in her life. She longs for Indian spiritualism and expresses her hatred against modern European civilization before Bashiam:

> Our world. The one in which I live. Things are battened down in it. Under concrete and mortar, all sorts of things. The land. Our instincts. The people who work in our factories, they've forgotten what fresh air is like. Our animals—we could learn from them, but we're Christian you know, an arrogant people so we deprive them of their rights. (*The Coffer Dams* 138)

Not only this the simmering volcano erupts, she continues:

> Deny them. Pretend they haven't got any. Then they don't know about sunshine or rain either, sometimes they can't move, poor things. We don't allow them to, in case, they yield us ounce less of their flesh. Where is

our instinct of pity? Blunted. We've cut ourselves off from heritage. We've forgotten what we know. Where can we turn to, to learn? A million years accumulating, and we know no better to kick it in the teeth. (*The Coffer Dams* 138)

She echoes Bashiam when she says, "there are some things which one has to do" (*The Coffer Dams* 138). These things become the responsibilities one has to perform thinking of a community. The vision of Helen is clear as she thinks more about the tribal settlements than about the coffer dams.

Mrs. Pickering in *The Nowhere Man* is a poor old divorcee and former nurse. She is the new woman who, without caring of racial antagonism, befriends Srinivas who feels isolation as he is stricken with two deaths, one of his favourite son Seshu and the other of Vasantha. She provides the need for a companionship. Social subsequent meetings conform their need for each other, as a sympathetic chord ties them into the bond of companionship and friendship. She goes to his building at his invitation and a sort of intimacy develops between them.

Laxman, Srinivas' son does not fail to notice the essential goodness of her character. First, he suspects Srinivas' sex-relationship and the claim that she may put forth. But, no sooner does he meet her than he changes his opinion about her. Srinivas replies to the question of his son concerning her identity:

"A friend," replied Srinivas "She shares the house with me. Have you not noticed how well kept it is? A pigsty" he said slyly, "no more." (*The Nowhere Man* 64)

She manages the house well and when Srinivas' income dwindles, she advises him to earn some money by converting the big mansion into cheap flats and letting them out to the poor. It is a great irony that Vasantha dreamt of the mansion being occupied by her children but her dream ends in smoke. Mrs. Pickering's plan increases his income and gives solace to his mind that he is helping the poor and needy. Like

Dr. Radcliffe, she is more concerned about a race of Cains that may be raised, if not already raised.

> Is that possible? Wondered Mrs. Pickering, whose mind was crammed with images, of the fallen weak and helpless, and of their sons, sons who not be content as Srinivas had been but could be trusted to raise Cain—if Cain had not in fact already been raised" (*The Nowhere Man* 312)

She does not feel guilty of Srinivas' death as she feels she has cared for him. Kamala Markandaya makes her say: "Blame myself," said Mrs. Pickering "Why should I? I cared for him," And indeed, that seemed to her to be the core of it" (*The Nowhere Man* 312)

If everyone cares for others as she has cared for Srinivas, all the holocaust in the name of race, religion and nationalism can be avoided. Their intimacy is the outcome of the association between two old lonely people. But, it does not mean, she fills the gap left by Vasantha. She cannot do so if she tries. She can care for his creature comforts but cannot become his sahadharma charini. Even in Mrs. Pickering's company, he feels spiritual loneliness but not physical solitude.

The Srinivas-Mrs. Pickering relationship in the novel is in sharp contrast to the Val-Caroline relationship in *Possession*. Markandaya inventively highlights the difference in terms of mature attitudes, shared human values and mutual sympathy. The ultimate loneliness of man is the common condition of Mrs. Pickering, a middle-aged widow, and Srinivas, a widower, about seventy. She, like Helen, builds the bridge of understanding on two separate banks of East and West. She is the most balanced and realistically realized British character ever created by the novelist. Her relationship with Srinivas is the relationship between the best of India and the best of Britain.

In *Two Virgins*, the characters of Lalitha and Saroja have been presented to symbolize two different attitudes to life. It is the beauty of Lalitha that inspires her to lead a modern life. Her character is a warning to young girls not to be misguided by their beauty. Like Faulkner's *Temple Drake*, she is promiscuous even in her virginity, salivating for ravishment. She is more beautiful than her sister Saroja. Being conscious of her beauty, she becomes a prey to narcissism. Kamala Markandaya presents her air:

> Lalitha had status, she had no husband yet, but everybody could see when she did. She would have more than her fair proportion. The young men's mothers sent them and the women came and smoke to Amma and pinched Lalitha's cheek, and Lalitha was demure, pressed her delicate feet together and cast down her eyes to show off her lashes, which were long and lustrous. (*Two Virgins* 13)

She loves her sister Saroja and with her, shares her feelings. Her deep love can be seen here in these lines:

> Lalitha called Saroja a sissy, a baby, a moon calf...she often brought things for Saroja, said nice things to her when she was in a giving mood, called her sweetness and pet and combed her hair, running it through her fingers and saying it was like silk. Saroja adored her sister in these moods, boasted about her to the girls at school. (*Two Virgins* 25)

She wishes to make her active, vivacious and smart like her. She is allergic to simplicity, which is poisonous to be advanced. She gives the tips of active life to her sister:

> You have to be quick. You have to seize your opportunity before it passes you by, you have to be quick with your answer if you want to get anywhere.... (*Two Virgins* 77)

City life allures her as she tells her mother, "It is barbaric not having a fridge" (*Two Virgins* 26). She is not convinced when her mother says that only film stars can afford such luxuries. In her opinion, these days fridge is not a luxury but a necessity. She feels herself in the seventh heaven when Miss Mendoza praises her beauty and certifies her suitability for a film career. Miss Mendoza introduces her to Mr. Gupta, film director who invites her to the city. She is lost in the enchantment of city life and on returning to the village, she complains of the terrible heat. She appreciates the comforts of the city life and tells her sister Saroja:

> There were electric fans in all the rooms with regulators marked from 1 to 5, 5 was full on. I always had them on 5, I loved the blades whirling around at the top speed though it created havoc with his papers (*Two Virgins* 163)

The balloon of her pride bursts when Mr. Gupta pumps too much air and makes her pregnant. She takes the fork to commit suicide but Saroja prevents her from doing so. She repents and votes for simplicity of Saroja who has a firm determination to keep away from the colourful temptation.

> "I wish I were you," said Lalitha Saroja stopped saying. "I too could be happy, said Lalitha. "Aren't you?" asked Saroja, "Of course," said Lalitha. (*Two Virgins* 209)

She is a virgin in a whorehouse. In spite of being deceived, exploited and harassed, her attraction for city life does not grow dim. She feels that the village "stifled her, her talent, her ambition. She intended to stay in the city where she belonged." She leaves the house quietly and goes away for good leaving a note asking her parents not "to search for her, which in case would be a waste of time because they could never find her" (*Two Virgins* 236).

In *The Golden Honeycomb*, the trio—Manjula, Mohini and Usha—has something in common. They come out breaking barriers to protest the British rule but in their limits. Of these, Manjula sows the seeds of royal rebellion. She insists on feeding her baby (born 1870) herself, contrary to the royal customs. She perceives the palace practice of restraining the royal mother from nursing her own child as an unwarranted denial of a basic human freedom. She protests but in vain. Even Bawajiraj II, who is loyal to the British Emperor, persuades her to accept his value system. She grieves to some extent and redresses her grievance too, yet, helplessly watches the Prince (the future Bawajiraj III) becoming loyal towards the British Emperor. She asks Mohini not to marry Bawajiraj III as she wishes to slap on the face of the British rule through her. Ultimately, she succeeds in her mission, for, Mohini now can bring up her son Rabindranath according to her sweet will.

The seeds sown by Manjula sprout and become saplings in the mind of Mohini. She is the only person before whom Bawajiraj III is helpless and behaves like a child before her. She is quite aware of her physical attractions, which she uses in ensnaring the Maharaja. Whenever she argues with him, she often emerges triumphant. She talks logically and makes him convince of the validity of her point of view. Bawajiraj falls in love with her and dreams of her. He wishes to marry her and wants to make her not only the queen of his heart but the real queen also. But, first of all, she is an Indian and being Indian she longs for freedom—freedom of thought, freedom of movement, freedom of all kinds—which the British have snatched from Indians. Hence, she does not want to marry Bawajiraj, as he is only a puppet in the hands of the Britishers. She feels satisfied merely to be his concubine, a status that guarantees her the freedom to bring up their son Rabindranath (1895), as she desires. Bawajiraj III pleads before her reminding the bond of love existing between him and Mohini.

"I beg you. Will you not marry me?"

"No"

"It would make me the happiest man alive."

"I can make you happy without that. I have no wish to be your second wife either." (*The Golden Honeycomb* 32)

Bawajiraj makes her realize of the child and asks her to be his real queen. But, she boldly rejects the offer saying: "I do not want to be your queen. I want to be free" (*The Golden Honeycomb* 32).

A new face of Mohini emerges in this rejection and reminds us of Milton who says: "Better to reign in Hell than serve in Heaven[9] Slavery shall be a sin for her. She would not like to be the queen at the cost of her freedom. She hates puppet-like image and is quite satisfied with her present condition of being a paramour. It is the cherished dream of every woman to be someone's wife but she kicks out the offer that promises her bright future of a queen. She wishes to live according to the values and norms which she has made herself and puts fingers in her ears as she does not want to listen to the music that will compel her to dance according to its tune. Bawajiraj III feels hurt about her decision and marries Shanti Devi, a colourless princess who bears him only daughters but no son.

Mohini is the symbol of Independence. She makes Bawajiraj III realize of the change in time. She is quite happy when he treats his people like a father. She says:

> For once in your life you are behaving like a father to your people. You are actually letting them keep a freedom of what's theirs instead of grabbing the whole lot for yourself and your bania friends. You ought to be pleased for their sake. (*The Golden Honeycomb* 465)

The seeds of new woman sown by Manjula sprout in Mohini but are grown into a full-length tree with ripe fruits in Usha. Usha inspires the fighters for freedom and plays the role of sheet anchor in Rabi's life. Usha who has fire in herself, fires the hearts of those who come in her touch. She reveals her anger saying that freedom struggle is not meant only for men. She stands by the suffering people and feels for them. In her attitude, she asserts the spirit of independence. She becomes a model to be followed by those women who do not want to confine themselves within four walls of their homes. They wish to prove that they can change and form the destiny of the country by their devotion to duty and active participation. Towards the end of the novel, she is seen with Rabi planning for future that will presumably result in their wedlock.

Usha and Rabindranath, the heir-apparent, make a perfectly compatible pair as comrades in their peaceful march towards the dawn of freedom. They not only symbolize the radical aspirations and idealism of an awakened people but also represent the royal commitment to the welfare of the people.

They are at once the custodian of culture and makers of history in modern India. They are not only the heralds of changing tradition but also the agents of change itself.

Valli in *Pleasure City* is neither downright traditional nor utter modern but is between the two extremes. She proves herself as a good daughter, good sister, good artist and above all good sales girl. She takes up her share of the household tasks. She is helpful to her parents and brothers—Muthu and Rikki. She is more co-operative to her foster brother Rikki than her real one Muthu. Rikki asks her to bring flowers to offer to Tully. She asks him, 'Did he (Tully) like the flower?' She receives the positive reply and presents flowers.

Her happiness knows no bound at the sight of Shalimar but Muthu is indifferent to it when he asks "What is the matter with you?," she replies to him, "The matter with you, said Valli, making her shoulders as sharp and scornful, as she could, is that you are simply incapable of appreciating beauty." (*Pleasure City* 115). Shalimar is beautiful for her. She wishes to wander again and again in Shalimar "among the flowers and lights and the gentry, within the crimson ropes of the cordon" (*Pleasure City* 115).

She is a good artist and takes part in the theatre. Carman helps much in her preparation and awakes confidence in her. She feels pleasure in dancing. She tells her foster brother Rikki: "Because when I dance it gives pleasure to—to whoever is watching, and the pleasure, reflects right back. I dance divinely then and I know I look divinely beautiful too, although, she heaved a sigh, "really I'm only passable—pretty" (*Pleasure City* 129).

Valli has no faith in the old adage- 'Home and hearth for woman.' She transcends the threshold of home and works as a sales assistant in the Shalimar Gift Shop and Emporium. She runs the shop soberly and successfully. She enjoys the new job as is clear from the following words:

> I am as blithe as a bird. It's a pleasure to be here, I just love it…. It makes such a nice change after slitting fish open the whole of one's life; she claimed. (*Pleasure City* 129)

Kamala Markandaya's words in the novel *The Pleasure City* "Airs that directors were like invisible diadems could also be sensed on their wives" (105) are quite applicable in case of Corinna who has come to Shalimar to meet her husband Tully. To Rikki, she looks like a horseman. "It was long and silky, a woman's flowing hair; the turban, and the shirt and trousers she was wearing, had led him to suppose a horseman" (*Pleasure City* 106)

She has great admiration for art. She asks Rikki to learn painting from her. She makes him look like a scholar. When he carries the equipments, she advises him to carry it not like a coolie but like a scholar. "Not like a coolie, Rikki I've told you before, like scholar, neatly, under one arm" (*Pleasure City* 131) Sometimes, he rebels against her absurd command but "these irksome bonds were cords of silk, to the radiant pupil he became" (*Pleasure City* 131), He sees the image of Mrs. Bridie in her.

Tully respects her and praises her saying "She has poise, confidence, command, comes up superbly from initial crouch to upright and hold the position. Balancing finely, she rides the skimming plank with her body, guides it in subtle diagonals, her first work is dazzling" (*Pleasure City* 131-32). But their marriage is of body, not of soul. There is a wide gulf that cannot be bridged. They are the two banks that cannot meet with each other. They can meet through water—bodily pleasure but their soul will remain segregated or sequestered.

> She shared his feelings, in more than one way. She too began to be conscious of distance or division. A sense of wedge between herself and her husband, more pronounced than she could remember, for she could not honestly pretend it had not manifested before. But hardened, while running alongside the incendiary unions that sequelled, as usual, their separation. The marriage is unsuccessful one. (*Pleasure City* 263)

There is isolation, alienation and frustration in place of companionship, love and mutual understanding in their relationship.

She is obstinate and does what she likes to do. Rikki wants to postpone the swimming for another day but she says: "I am leaving tomorrow, it is now or never, Rikki" (*Pleasure City* 305). He foresees the danger and thinks: "If she had been a boat he would have beached her high and dry, out of harm's way. As it was he watched her walking, slightly lopsided with the weight of the board, down to the sea" (*Pleasure City* 305). She is not afraid as she feels there is nothing she cannot handle. But no sooner does she realize the truth that she is being swept out to sea than she screams. Rikki goes after her, in the wake of the crazy diagonals in which cross currents were dragging her.

She realizes her mistake and repents for it. "I am sorry, Toby. About Rikki, I mean. It was unforgivable. I must have been mad" (*Pleasure City* 317). She fails to go into the depth and to peep into the hearts of Indians. "She would never know Rikki, or perhaps the country he was bound up with, were equally outside her reach" (*Pleasure City* 318).

Her husband goes to the airport to see her off. She talks about Rikki and feels happy to know that he is mending. At last, both of them kiss each other but they do not feel the warmth of the passion of love. He holds this country responsible for this alienation and coldness in their relationship.

> When they kissed at the barren their lips were affectionate, but cool. So cool and unimpassioned that Tully momentarily rebelled, furiously charging the country with extracting its last pound of flesh; but as this was not true, as indeed he knew, the fury died even as it was kindled. (*Pleasure City* 319)

Thus, Corinna presents a weak image of the relationship. She is self-satisfied and wishes to live in her own world without caring for others.

'Brain wave, your wife's' are the words of Boyle in praise of Mrs. Contractor. Really, she is brain wave as she manages all the activities of Shalimar. She feels "If Shalimar was a little world of its own, there was a little world within that world that was also rounding out nicely" (Pleasure City 151). She is very practical in her approach and amiable in behaviour. She believes in commercialization of things and attracts more and more customers providing them facilities for their enjoyment. She has strict control over the staff members and tells them frankly: "If no one comes to Shalimar, let me tell you, you will all be out of a job" (*Pleasure City* 150). She advises her guests what to do, where to go and what to eat. She is very polite in her treatment when the guests thank her for her precious advice and care. She tells them:

> Would you not do the same for me if I were a stranger in your country? No, no it is nothing, it is simply do unto others. (*Pleasure City* 151)

Women are not inferior to men as they are entering every field of life. They are proving that they are superior to men. Mrs. Lovat in *Pleasure City* is no exception. She is wholly devoted to her profession of writing. She wishes to write a book about India. She has booked in for three months at special reduced rate in Shalimar. She comes in touch with Rikki who tells her the old stories—tales from his childhood and sea lore. She says: "It is just that your country fascinates me. I'd like to find out as much as I can, that's all" (*Pleasure City* 154).

The books she writes about India are admired everywhere except in India. She complains and is unable to understand why her novels are not liked. "I cannot figure out why; she said. She would not let it worry her too much, but it was hurtful" (*Pleasure City* 156). She feels more comfortable in Rikki's company. She is indebted to him for his active co-operation. When she goes away, she does not forget to wish good health for Rikki.

> I want to finish my book. And don't be surprised; she said archly. If you find yourself in it. (*Pleasure City* 333)

Kamala Markandaya's novels are primarily a study of the basic fact of awakening of feminine consciousness. They mirror a new awareness of fulfilments of feminine identity.

Her female protagonists are seeking self-fulfilment through self-expression without losing their basic personality. Rejecting the conventional role of subjugation and self-denial, they have raised the flag of new woman in their hands to make the male-oriented society realise of their integral position and importance. A new awakening has been commenced and now, they do not wish merely to be studied through any set methodology. Kamala Markandaya has attempted a reassessment of what a woman in the Indian set up aspires to be and her female protagonists like Rukmani, Ira, Mira, Roshan, Nalini, Helen, Lalitha, Mohini, Usha, Valli etc., who have shown that they are not inferior to their male counterparts in any way, prove Kamala Markandaya's viewpoint. The image of new woman emerges in them though not proper yet in making.

## Notes and References

1. "Emergence of New Woman in Indian Fiction" *Feminism and Literature* edited by Veena Noble Dass (New Delhi: Prestige Books), 220.

2. "Concept of The New Woman" *The New Woman in Indian English Fiction* (New Delhi: Creative Books), 17-18.

3. *The New Woman In Indian English Fiction* (New Delhi: Creative Books), 20-21.

4. Shanta Krishnaswamy, *The Woman in Indian Fiction in English* (New Delhi: Ashish Publishing House, 1984) VI.

5. "Deconstructing Feminism: Nectar in a Sieve and The Phenomenon of Change," *Indian Women Novelists* Set II, Vol. II, ed. by R.K. Dhawan (New Delhi: Prestige Books) 143.

6. "Significance of The Title Nectar in a Sieve", Ramesh K. Srivastava, *Six Indian Novelists,* 92-93.

7. G.R. Taneja, "Deconstructing Feminism: Nectar in a Sieve and the Phenomenon of Change," *Indian Women Novelists*, Set II, Vol. II, ed. R.K. Dhawan (New Delhi: Prestige Books), 143.

8. Iyengar, *Indian Writing In English*, 448.

9. Milton, *Paradise Lost,* Book I, line 263.

# An In-depth Analysis of the Image of Woman

## 5

None but Time knows what is hidden in its womb. It makes unexpected expected and expected unexpected. A man behaves normally when it is expected that he will behave abnormally and reverses the whole equation by behaving abnormally when normal behaviour is expected from him. In ordinary life, one sees a man outwardly and forms an image but never sees him inwardly as he is incapable to search out the waves of real motives and feelings that are rising in the mind. A man who looks fine, calm and normal outwardly may be disturbed, stormy and abnormal inwardly. It is, really, difficult to enter and penetrate the mind as well as the heart of a man. Yet, an in-depth analysis can be formed on the basis of his talks, ideas, doings, behaviour, etc. The present chapter is an attempt to make an in-depth analysis of Kamala Markandaya's women who divulge some peculiarities like neurosis, Platonic love, sex and sensuality etc. Neurosis, in the words of Alfred H. Moller, is caused by bottled up feelings, because when people repress their feelings, they repress their memories and traumatic experiences.[1] More or less, the society is responsible for neurosis as it compels a person against his or her wish to suppress instinctual urges, feelings and longings for the free exercise of will for the sake of maintaining its ideals and foundations. If he or she is not capable of opposing the societal sanctions openly, he or she searches an option for her protest in neurosis. Women suffer more than men on account of social norms and moral code, which are imposed against their wishes. M. Rajeshwar writes in this connection:

Women are mercilessly denied opportunities for open expression of their true feelings in the tradition-bound Indian society. In this respect and in many other respect they are at great disadvantage when compared to men.[2]

Kamala Markandaya believes that "the process of creating writing reveals depths in the mind which are of universal application."[3] She has treated the neurotic phenomenon in the Indian context by creating extremely interesting characters. She wishes to prove that society is often indifferent and vindictive towards sensitive and aggrieved souls while it should come forward for their help, as they need its love, affection and sympathy.

Platonic friendship is a contested concept that includes friendships between men and women without the touch of physical love. Such friendships are rare and difficult to maintain because of the temptation of falling into personal familiarities, which give birth to the debatable relation. Kamala Markandaya has beautifully introduced not only the Platonic friendship but also true love, which include intellectual congeniality and spiritual sympathy as well as physical attraction. She believes true love desires only to give. She prefers true love to marriage devoid of love. Sex and sensuality are a part of life. In order to accept life, one has to accept sex which is the primary drive only next to hunger. Mrs. Mary Wood Allen writes in this connection:

> Instead, then, of looking at sex circumscribed, and perhaps as something low and vulgar, to be thought of and spoken of only with whispers or questionable mirth, we should see that sex is God's divinest gift to humanity, the power through which we come into the nearest likeness to Himself—the function by which we become creators and transmitters of our powers of body, mind and soul."[4]

Kamala Markandaya is aware of the fact that all the sweet ties of home and family depend upon sex that contributes in having the dear family life with its anniversaries of weddings and birthdays. It is through sex that the desolate of the earth are set in families. It would be better if one regards it with reverent thought and considers it sacred to the highest purposes.

It is a psychological truth that a man feels highly obliged and pays respect to that man who helps him in his need and saves him from emotional isolation. He keeps his image in his mind realizing indebtedness to him. The same happens with Rukmani in *Nectar in a Sieve*. She has the image of Dr. Kenny somewhere in her mind. It was Dr. Kenny who wiped out emotional frustration not only of her but of her daughter also by his treatment. She keeps his image in her mind and is in love without conscious of it. She suppresses but sometimes her mask falls off. She has an emotional attachment for him and thinks him no less than God. When she comes to know that Dr. Kenny has returned, she drops her marketing and buys a garland of flowers and flies to him as a beloved would to a lover. She unlocks her heart:

> "My lord, my benefactor," I cried "Many a time I have longed to see you. Now, at last you came, and I bent down to kiss his feet, shod as they were in leather shoes. He withdrew them quickly and told me to get up."
> (*Nectar in a Sieve* 36)

She develops a Platonic love for him and enjoys his image in her mind. But, first of all, she is a traditional woman who is conscious of her duties to her husband and the family. She suppresses her feelings and never gives them words to come out. For the sake of her family, she has to be blackmailed by Kunthi who threatens her of exposing her relations with Dr. Kenny to Nathan. She feels a burden on her heart as she feels guilty conscious but when she comes to know about the illicit relations of her husband with Kunthi, she feels the burden lightened.

Though *Nectar in a Sieve* is a study of Rukmani's courage and patience to face life's blasts, there are some moments that she enjoys and cannot forget. She does not like to remember the scene of her first night but "I prefer to remember, sweeter, fuller, when I went to my husband matured in mind as well as in body, not as a pained and awkward child as I did on that first night" (*Nectar in a Sieve* 8-9).

She enjoys the memory of some unforgettable moments that gave the fruit of love. An equally invigorating moment in her life comes on the day of Deepawali when she unites with her husband offering herself wholly:

> I stretched myself out beside him, close to him in the darkness, and as we touched he turned abruptly towards me. Words died away, the listening air was very still, the black night waited. In the straining darkness I felt his body moving with desire, his hands on me were trembling, and I felt my senses opening like flower to his urgency. I closed my eyes and waited, waited in the darkness while my being filled with a wild ecstatic fluttering waited for him to come to me (*Nectar in a Sieve* 61).

Mira in *Some Inner Fury* is great in her sacrifice but this sacrifice leaves many questions unsolved. Is it necessary for Mira to leave Richard? She loves Richard as Richard, not as a Britisher. Why does she see a Britisher in him now? If she can see Kit and Govind as individuals, why does she not see Richard, whom she loves so much, as a man and not a Britisher? Richard asks her "Has it infected you too...all this 'Your people' and 'my people?' (*Some Inner Fury* 138). Though she replies to him in negative, yet, at some unconscious level, something must have happened to her, for the night before the trial, she asks him, "Do you believe Hickey? ...do you believe this English man's word against mine" (*Some Inner Fury* 264). So by the time of trial, she is totally committed in her stand, and is certainly not neutral. If she had been neutral, she would have chosen Richard, her lover, not Govind, the destroyer. She rises above the self, and plunges into the redeeming fire of the national movement.

National movement aggravates the fire of love in their hearts to such an extent as they go off on a honeymoon, part of the way by car, and later by any mode of transport they fancy. They go to the tip of the land at Kanyakumari with nothing more than a single suitcase between them, eating and drinking wherever they could, finding simple shelter along the route, making love and drinking life to the lees. While taking a naked bath in the sea or basking in the sun, Richard becomes "a creature of gold," (*Some Inner Fury* 196) his body turns to "a pale gold" and his hair glinting golden against the skin, "the skin as tight and firm as a silken sheath" (*Ibid.*). The warmth of his flawless sculptured body could "make you melt, or set you on fire and burn with an incandescent heat itself" (*Some Inner Fury* 197).

They love, talk of love and drink love to the last drop. In changing and moving atmosphere, they are lost in each other's arms and act as unmarried husband and wife. Richard talks of 'fever' and 'ache' and begs for intercourse on the uninhibited coast. This is the culmination of love; he says:

> "We're alone," he said, holding me still, "Quite alone," and the skies were empty, the sands were bare, I listened and there was only the sound of the sea.

> "You see," he said softly, "There is nothing and no one. No one but us."

> "Slowly my senses awoke and responded, the buds of feeling swelled and opened one by one. In the trembling silence, I heard the blood begin its clamour, felt its frantic irregular beat, then the world fell away, forgotten in this wild abandoned rhythm, lost in the sweep and surge of love." (*Some Inner Fury* 198-99)

Richard coats the honey on the face of the moon. Both feel highly cheered and satisfied. Both of them promise to be together all the time.

> "I am so happy with you darling. You're wonderful to be with—not just now, all the time."

> "I wish we could be together all the time."

> "We shall be, soon." (*Some Inner Fury* 199)

The tensions between Sarojini and Dandekar in *A Silence of Desire* are broadened and deepened when Dandekar picks up a photograph that falls out of an exercise book. A feeling of jealousy that is in his subconscious, emerges and starts its action "A married woman did not have men friends who were not known to the husband, the family one of the girl's idols perhaps a teacher, a film actor?" (*A Silence of Desire* 34).

He meets Rajam whose gregariousness soon reveals that she had not visited Sarojini. He feels that there is mistake somewhere. Doubts multiply doubts. At the remark of Joseph, "Women are sly cats, you never know what they're going to be up to next" (*A Silence of Desire* 37). Dandekar, though he disagrees, he feels "dispirited, vulnerable, and somewhere around the perimeter of his mind, seeking entry, snuffled the thought: all women are the same" (*A Silence of Desire* 37).

She knows well Dandekar's western frame of mind and scientific attitude. She is conscious that her going to the Swamy will be disapproved but "she unconsciously protests against him just as Tara protested against her pedantic husband Brihaspati by physically running away with Soma in the Rigvedic myth. Sarojini does it differently, in a manner that is sanctioned by tradition and achieves the desired effect. In her unconscious, the Swamy plays the lover and the father at the same time."[5]

She has psychological reason for sticking to faith healing. She knows that her grandmother and mother had been hospitalized. The fear psychosis has tormented her and searches another way to avoid certain death. That she believes in faith-healing, as a part of the Eastern philosophy is not true. She needs a person to make her sure that she should not be afraid of knives and doctor, and any psychologist can provide her with that much of balance and stability. Barrier of East and West is no bar in psychological treatment. She goes to meet the Swamy who attends to her neurotic need for love and self-importance. What he ministers actually is not the alleviation of the pain that her body experiences but the pain her psyche experiences—the pain born of a sense of neglect and worthlessness. A temporary euphoria neutralizes the physical pain for the time being. The Swamy's image is internalized and going to him becomes something of an addiction. M. Rajeshwar opines "she lacks the necessary intellectual resources to discriminate between the needs of her body and the needs of her psyche. She therefore develops the false belief that "without faith I shall not be healed."[6]

There is a selfish motive in her visit to the Swamy whom she thinks that he will cure her of her growth (tumour). For this, she adopts every kind of subterfuge—lying, cheating, even stoops down to steal from her own house compelled by her hypnotic faith in the Swamy's power of healing. No attachment can be pure if it demoralizes a human being in his or in other's eyes and Sarojini, when she tries to propagate her Eastern belief, actually sounds phony. It seems that she has never loved her husband in real sense otherwise she should not behave in this very confusing and complex way. She never feels that Dandekar is a part of her body and soul and when she comes back to the normal routine, it shows no extraordinary feelings and no reaching of emotional heights. She takes it simply a return to her wifely duties.

Caroline in *Possession* exploits Val physically as well as spiritually in the name of promoting his artistic talent. She uses him for her selfish motives. She shows her absolute possession over him. She removes Ellie and Annabel whom she thinks her rivals who are trying to snatch Val from her. First of all, she removes Ellie when she finds her pregnant by Val. Now, she sees a rival in Annabel whom she thinks second Ellie who has fallen in love with him. She repeats the story of Ellie to Annabel to make her aware of the tragedy that she will also suffer and come to the same tragic end like Ellie. She picks out the clipping and shows to Annabel "four lines of small print about a pregnant woman, an unemployed domestic, reaching the end of her tether" (*Possession* 206) She incites her to leave Val by appealing to her sense of racialism. But, she talks like a neurotic when she fails to defeat the Swamy. "Valmiki is yours now, but he has been mine. One day he will want to be mine again. I shall take care to make him want me again: and on that day I shall come back to claim him" (*Possession* 232). Though hopeless, she does not accept her defeat. At the Swamy's asking "If the day comes," she says, "Of course, it will come" (*Possession* 233).

In *Possession,* there is possession of sex and nothing else. The remote is in the hands of Caroline who makes Val dance to her whims. She should treat him like her son but she treats him only a means to satisfy her lust. Val is fed up but is helpless. Though he turns his attention towards Ellie and Annabel, he has to sleep with Caroline in the same bed at night. Anasuya says:

> Meanwhile, in that eerie household, as far as I could gather Caroline and Valmiki continued to sleep in the same bed at night. By day it was Valmiki and Annabel. (*Possession* 199)

Val makes Ellie pregnant and enjoys sex with Annabel. Anasuya presents minutely the scene where she finds Annabel and Valmiki:

> Spread-eagled on a rug in front of the electric fire lay Annabel. Valmiki covered her. They were closely locked from mouth to loins until the firm white legs flared away from under him. Both were naked, and their bodies moved as if they were a unity, with a beautifully articulated urgent rhythm... I was shivering, partly from cold, partly no doubt from what I had seen: yet why? I had seen enough fucking in the overcrowded desperate hovels of India, and had not developed any emphatic attitudes either way.... (*Possession* 194)

Kamala Markandaya is rather frank and forward in describing sex and sensuality in her works. But, she is never vulgar or immodest. She enjoys its artistic flavour naturally without any ambiguity. How accurately and minutely, she has described the first night of the newly married couple Ravi and Nalini in *A Handful of Rice.*

> "The sudden darkness was blinding. He groped his way back, and feet his outstretched hand touch warm smooth skin, her self-bare nape beneath the upsweat voluptuous coils of hair. Instantly his senses leapt into life, he could hardly contain himself. He pressed her back on the bed and began caressing her, thrusting aside the filmy hampering folds of the muslin sari into which she had

changed until he could feel her body and it was everything he wanted, warm, soft, long, fine, supple legs, a belly that arched under his hand, and a skin like satin—he heard himself cry out as he covered her, spreading her thighs to receive him. He did not know if he was hurting her—he could not have stopped if he was. He heard her sharp indrawn breath, but otherwise she lay passively under him.

In the morning—he looked for it—there was blood on the bed. (*A Handful of Rice*  64)

Here Kamala Markandaya uses the blood on the bed to show Nalini's virginity. It seems that she is crazy about this crimson colour. She shows that the passive Nalini, as the time passes, becomes active willing female who has become expert in the art of love-making.

Now she was beginning to respond to him, making love as he, encouraged by her willingness, thought her to learning to abandon herself, to give her body without shame to him to do, with as he willed, so that now instead of a passive submission they came together joyously. (*A Handful of Rice* 66)

Sex is a taboo in lower middle class family. Even the members do not talk about in daylight. Sex is unmentionable subject by day, despite the frenzies of night. Nalini's husband regrets that she does not talk of sex, although she fully co-operates in the game of love-making. One night, her husband returns home very late. She weeps and then after making peace with him, she goes to sleep. One desire is silenced, other desire arises—full-blooded and passionate. Her husband turns, starts caressing her slowly and waits until she is ready for him. Kamala Markandaya is superb in presenting the first night but she is wonderful in describing the fore-play of love-making.

His wife, he thought with a surge of possession, his to have, his to hold...his excitement grew, externals fell away, there was nothing at all in the world beyond this feeling between him and this woman. (*A Handful of Rice* 77)

This love-making remains unconsummated as Varma wakes up "The glow so quickly kindled as rapidly died, leaving the quiet residue of incompletion" (*A Handful of Rice* 77).

Kamala Markandaya reveals sex and sensuality without using sexual words. Under shawl and coverlets, every thing is possible. This is what she wishes to convey. Puttanna manages to impregnate Thangam for the second time in a house where there is no privacy.

> While Puttanna who could scarcely support the child he already had, who seldom had any privacy in the quarters he shared away and asleep with Apu and Jayamma, had somehow succeeded under cover of shawls and coverlets in impregnating his wife who had not imagined she would conceive with a baby still at the breast. (*A Handful of Rice* 91)

Jayamma, mother of Nalini, is neurotic as she suppresses her hunger for sex. In spite of giving birth to many children, she is starved. She wishes to be controlled and crushed by masculine power. Apu could not give what she wished. That is why, she becomes neurotic as she suffers from fit of sex when she sees a man like Ravi who is masculine to every inch. Outwardly, she suppresses it but inwardly, she feels the heat of its flames and aches with sweet pain. Kamala Markandaya very subtly describes her condition:

> What troubled her, she liked to believe, was that she had done it: she, who had been brought up to respect every living being as the fragmentation of an eternal God. But going deeper, which she could hardly being herself to do, she knew that what really troubled her was the lust that had risen in her like a tide, the surging exultation that glutted her as she felt her blows falling on his flesh. (*A Handful of Rice* 55)

The ideal image of masculine power is mirrored in Ravi and she longs for him but never opens her mouth:

> She shivered a little thinking of Ravi's masculinity: and there was even the seed of a thought in her mind, though she would not let it grow, that in her daughter's

place she would have welcomed her wounds. (*A Handful of Rice* 188)

Ravi, who is drunk, comes and asks Jayamma about his wife Nalini. She tells him she does not know where she is. Quite contrary to expectations, unexpected happens. He loses his balance and control over himself. The serpent stands erect and bites Jayamma who opposes in the beginning but enjoys its sting. Jayamma might have loved to quench the fire that arose from the liver. Ravi was aware of it: "Why should I? You've wanted it for months, for years. All the time you lay with your husband. Every time you looked at me." (*A Handful of Rice* 221). She struggles and calls him a 'Ruffian Thug' (*Ibid.*). She tries to come out from his masculine grip but fails. "She was struggling. He held her and his excitement grew with her movements; her arms and breasts were soft and pulpy under his hands" (*Ibid.*).

He is encouraged by her former activities of looking at him with sexual desire. "You like it," he said, his mouth rough on her nipples, bringing them up hard and erect. "Do you think your body doesn't give you away? Do you think I don't know how you have been starved?" (*A Handful of Rice* 221).

He is deaf and dumb to Jayamma, and with his strong hammer, he strikes on iron. The hot iron smelts and is cooled off:

> But her face was luminous in the moonlight, her eyes wide and brilliant, the whites showing, closing, and he was lost, in soft enveloping flesh that tossed away past and future, wiping out pain and unhappiness, and all his waking and sleeping terrors. (*A Handful of Rice* 221)

Many critics have wished that Kamala Markandaya should not write this rape scene and consider it a blot. They think that she has repeated the mistake of Jane Austen who, in her novel *Pride and Prejudice*, has described the elopement scene of Lydia and Wickham. But if circumstances are considered from the psychological point of view, the rape scene becomes a natural corollary of deep veiled desires. They will have to accept the necessity of this scene. Jayamma is starved desiring for the food, which is provided by Ravi. This is the food that gives taste to both—Receiver and Giver and satisfies the hunger. Ravi is drunk and loses the sense of right or wrong. He has already seen her mother-in-law watching him and staring his body. Now, though not knowingly, he grasps her parts of the body, feels the electric shock, which neutralizes his mind and is lost in them. He satisfies her lust but along with it, he relieves himself by giving vent to his anger on her body. The storm of his anger blasts on Jayamma and there is complete silence when it is over. Jayamma's heart longs for body but she never expected her inner desire would be fulfilled in such forced rape. It is quite surprising that Ravi is ashamed of his act but she is not. She tells Ravi who asks her to forgive him.

> "What for—last night?' she said, and stared at him. 'Do you think I care about that? Who cares what goes on between four walls?" (*A Handful of Rice* 223)

Helen in *The Coffer Dams* realizes unity with her own true self through her union with Bashiam. She gives herself to him and in return, experiences mental peace and fulfilment that she often misses in her union with her husband. For the first time in her life, she feels a sense of belonging and develops a sense of universal inclusiveness.

> I belong, I'm not alone. Everything is a part of me, and I'm a part of everything. And just a pop-up card-board figure.... And felt the release as spoke, a peace that was to do with her mind as consummation had been for her body, the fusion making her whole in a way that she could not recall having achieved before. (*The Coffer Dams* 139)

But any such union can never be permanent until or unless it is based on mutual help and comfort like the relationship of Srinivas—Mrs Pickering (*The Nowhere Man*). Eleena J. Kalinnikova observes: "The arrival of 'sophisticated' Helen to the hut of 'dense' Bashiam and their physical intimacy are nothing else but Kamala's contribution to freudism."[7]

Miss K. Madhavi Menon and A.V. Krishna Rao write in this connection:

> ...The Helen-Bashiam affair is dictated by Helen's inner urge to give out, her felt need to redeem herself and her people, as it were as well as by Bashiam's casual avidity to possess Helen in order to prove himself, often dismissed as a mere 'Jungli' or a half-caste tribal by the British and the Indians alike."[8]

The devil of commercialism takes Clinton in the grip, washes his brain and fills it with the thought of concrete and mortar. For him, human relations have no importance. He scolds his wife Helen for favouring the tribal people. But, Helen pays him in the same coin. She befriends Bashiam without caring for Clinton who negates her feelings. Clinton himself, not observing it constructs a dam on the path of Helen's feelings and they select a different course. Their relations are snapped. Clinton is jealous and over possessive and cannot see anything far being snatched away. On account of this, he tries to dominate Helen and sees her with anger mixed with hunger for body. It results in near raping of his wife, as her heart was not in the act at that time. Kamala Markandaya frankly uses the confrontational act of Clinton to convey at once symbolically his over possessiveness and jealous male chauvinism as well as his coercive need to assert his authority.

Sex is a religion for Kamala Markandaya. She worships it and loves it. It is not a lust but a key to open the door of true love that leads to the home of Eternal pleasure. She sketches Vasantha (*The Nowhere Man*) who is a pleasing girl "a pretty girl who wouldn't be prettier still if she were not quite so thin, but then who wouldn't be after she'd been through, poor child" (*The Nowhere Man* 129).

Kamala Markandaya relishes in presenting the first night. Whether she does it to please the western readers or not but one thing is clear that, in her description, she is accurate in presenting a living picture. When marriage ceremony is over, Srinivas meets his wife Vasantha who is looking like rose. He loves her, stares her and takes her in her arms and, ultimately fills the vital juice in her.

> When he touched his bride he was so suffused with love for her—for flesh and spirit that were so beautifully conjoined—that he could not hold back. Forgive me, forgive me, some part of his brain cried, but soon he was lost, flooded with sensation which obliterated mind. Through it all, she complied. Her body opened for him, accepted his. That was the sum of it. The exultance that he demanded, the heartbeat and tumult, were all absent. It will come, he panted, striving as he had striven in his dreams, sinking himself deep into her flesh until he touched the pulp of her womb. But, it did not, then or ever.

In the morning, there was blood on the sheets. It seemed like a symbol to him. He showed it to her, full of tenderness, which replaced the night's urgencies.

"Your virginity," he said gently, "surrendered to me. Immaculate, unsullied by anyone or anything before." She gazed at him, compromised, uncompromising, the look he learned to know very well later, in England.

> "That is the physical fact of the matter." She said. (*The Nowhere Man* 157)

Mrs. Fletcher in *The Nowhere Man* often behaves like neurotic and suffers from the qualms of Christian conscience. After knowing the innate goodness of Srinivas, she is restless and tense at the thought of the pain that she has caused to him. It is he who comforts her by his presence at a time when she feels alone. She fails to know why her son Fred is hostile to him. She is sure that Fred has caused the damage through his involvement in the inhuman act. She feels so much concerned about the misdeeds of her son, that she offers prayers that he may be granted Christian love and understanding. She consoles Srinivas reflecting her genuine concern for humanity.

> You don't want to pay any attention to Fred. He doesn't know what he's talking about. You've got as much right to live here as he has. More.—Even if you weren't born in this country, Mr. Srinivas, you belong

here and don't let anyone convince you different (*The Nowhere Man* 174)

In *Two Virgins*, Kamala Markandaya portrays a growing young girl's secret longing for sex. She opines that the girl dreams of sex, sets image in her mind and takes pleasure in intellectual sex that influences her thoughts and activities. One of such descriptions which is an exercise in the portrayal of a growing young girl's secret yearning for sex, is thus:

> His hands were terrible; they were puffy and fat and they looked like a bunch of bananas, Jaya said. What terrible things those fingers, could do if they reached up under your skirts. Saroja closed up her thighs and asked exactly, but Jaya only said it was not to be described. Jaya's eyes shone when she told; she was older than Saroja, but in the same class. Saroja could not interpret that sheer disturbed her, made her feel she was missing out. (*Two Virgins* 79)

It is the latent sex that is revealed when one feels and is suppressed through intellectual intercourse. Saroja is able to suppress it on the moral ground. She will never repeat the story of Lalitha. That is why she manages to remain a virgin whereas her sister ceases to be one. She boldly rejects the attractive enticement of Devraj who attempts to make a pass at her. She foresees his evil designs in his attempt to woo her.

> He came close. He touched her. Please, he said, Saroja leapt up. Her flesh was molten. She knew what he was asking. She knew where it ended. She had dragged her bloated gravid sister out of the bog; she had seen the bloody pulp of the baby. Take your hands off me, she cried,...what do you take me for, she screamed, a virgin in your whorehouse. (*Two Virgins* 245)

Owing to the strength of her character, she does not fall to the snares set by the snarer Devraj for her.

*Two Virgins* is a highly educative novel for those girls who fall an easy prey to the glamour of the modern film world and fail to realize the serious hazards in life. Lalitha's story is a glaring instance of the tragedy of the modern women. What W.B. Yeats said, is quite true:

> It's certain that fine women eat
> A crazy salad with their meat
> Whereby the Horn of plenty is undone.[9]

Beautiful girls who think of physical beauty as an end in itself, commit mistakes. They enjoy this hallucination of being beautiful. By dint of beauty, they dream of winning the whole world and wish to rule over the people. Their imagination soars high in the sky when someone praises them for their beauty. They are poor in real sense as they are devoid of the real beauty—beauty of character and beauty of thought. Beauty is more important than virtue for them. Lalitha who, being proud of her beauty, falls an easy prey to the glamourous world commits the same mistake. She hates village where she feels like a fish out of water and loves city where she is lost in the dazzling lights. She has become so addicted to city life that even after the loss of her virginity at the hands of Mr. Gupta, she does not leave its temptations and hence, leaves her village for good in order to take the strong doses of facilities in high quantity.

Kamala Markandaya sprinkles crimson colour on her women characters. Some crimson droplets also fall on the women characters of *The Golden Honeycomb*, which is her experiment in historical novel. The hero of the novel Rabi develops a tender love for Janaki who works in the Palace garden. She has "the freedom of a bird" (*The Golden Honeycomb* 220) and her youth overflows from the tight clothes. Her ribs and rips can be seen through the clothes that give a shape to her beautiful cuts of her physical parts. Rabi is enamoured by them. When he goes to Delhi, she accompanies him. He buys a yellow sari for her but in the meantime, she disappears mysteriously and nothing is known about her.

Jaya, whom he meets in Bombay, gives him an erotic pleasure. Jaya's husband has been imprisoned for five years, so she is leading a secluded life. When she meets Rabi, she finds him injured. She invites him to her hut. Soon the sexual serpent starts crawling, bites them and both of them roll over each other in the dead silence of the night. Jaya takes it easy, feels satisfied and co-operates fully in satisfying him sexually.

A magnetic personality coupled with stout body normally arrests the attention of fair sex. Vimla, the Dewan's elder daughter, is drawn towards him and unsuccessfully attempts to lure him but her father comes to know about it and he immediately arranges for her marriage with a Brahmin boy of the neighbouring state. She remains unsatisfied in not making him of hers, suppresses her feelings and obeys her father though reluctantly. Her younger sister Usha develops affection for Rabi, which results into true love. It is quite surprising that the same father who hindered the path of Vimala, allows concessions to his younger daughter Usha for her amour patriae. She daringly moves and enjoys with Rabi.

In *Pleasure City*, childless Mrs. Bridie admires and adores Rikki. Rikki in turn idealizes her and prefers her to all. Bridie-Rikki relationship develops like Oedipus complex. Being a child, he lies in her lap and feels her bosom—so flat...not at all like the full globes of his mother. There is something somewhere that he compares their bosoms and prefers Bridie to his mother. Mr. Bridie follows his wife in death and is buried with her.

> They were buried together, on the same day, in the small cemetery where Indian soil had taken care, over three centuries, of the bones of the missionary English (*Pleasure City* 16).

But, it is more surprising than the fact of their burial that Rikki expresses his anger at this and tears pour down on his face. "You shouldn't have buried them like that," he reproved. "She could never bear him to touch her, you know" (*Pleasure City* 16). Her image always haunts his mind even after her death.

Amma, who is a little selfish, feels glad and relieved when she gets Rikki back from Mrs. Bridie. She considers her to be her rival for him as she feels Mrs. Bridie has snatched him from her.

> Amma was glad. Let no one say she rejoiced over death, never that, no, but it was a relief to have her foster son

from that Mrs. Bridie. The stringy woman had lured him away, she felt, more often than was fair, and a little too often for her liking. Because, was he or was he not a fisherman born? Besides which it was pleasing to have the affectionate clear-eyed child by her; restored, she put it to herself, to the bosom of her family." (*Pleasure City* 17)

Just as a beloved feels highly elated when she sees her lover, in the same way, the sight of Rikki always cheers her. "Rikki, she hailed, the sight of him always cheered her. 'There you are at last! Whatever kept you?" (*Pleasure City* 17)

Due to influence of materialism one thinks of body, not of soul. Body is more important than soul. The first thing that strikes the mind is body. Corinna who arrives to see her husband, meets him coldly and remains isolated engrossed in her own world. Her husband Tully, when he comes to know of her arrival, feels elated and flies to her dreaming of enjoying her lovely, plangent flesh. What an irony! To meet after a long gap and dream of flesh, not of feelings!

Corinna had gone to bed, earning early retirement after the most charming genuflections that had everyone, virtually yearning to construct a litter. She would probably be asleep; but would always wake, and make available, to him her lovely, plangent flesh. (*Pleasure City* 114)

Rikki catches the sight of Tully and his wife who are standing face to face, not speaking, not touching. Ego factor makes them dumb. She is quite surprised at her husband's preference for Avalon. He asks her whether she likes living here. She does not wish to answer but says so, so. His hands start working. They stop exchange of words. Their bodies search for food to satisfy hunger. Satisfying physical urge is the definition of mere lust, not of true love. "...lovely arms inviting. 'Come to bed, darling.' Luckily he never needed a second invitation; and the molten experience made it easier for both of them, postponing franker exchanges" (*Pleasure City*, 124).

Such sexual act is different from the sexual act of Rukmani and Nathan (*Nectar in a Sieve*) who co-operate when they are in celestial mood and become one soul out of two bodies.

It seems that she has come only for bodily pleasures. She finds him marvelous and positively blooming. She asks no question and is lost with him.

> 'Don't know—about you—never have—but between kisses, lips full on his, stopping him up. He getting clear, pining her flat so he can look at her.
>
> 'But what?'
>
> 'But I don't care. Does for me, darling. Totally. Beautifully. —Toby?'
>
> Inviting him again. He accepting, as he wants to. Every sign, as she says; and the encounter has never been less than delightful. However, it has to stop. Limits for a man, though not, she makes it clear, for Corinna. (*Pleasure City* 253-54)

Thus, an in-depth study of Kamala Markandaya's works reveals that men and women discrimination prevails in male-oriented Indian society. All sorts of limitations and restrictions are imposed merely on women. Men who belong to the privileged class are supposed to be superior to and more powerful than women. Women belonging to the weaker sex, suppress their sexual urge due to inhibition and modesty, which results in neurosis. The desire of moth for the star, a sort of Platonic love lurking from the hidden recesses of their heart clamours for fulfilment, when it is denied it erupts in Freudian lava. Kamala Markandaya reveals her concern for their emancipation as they are not only worst sufferers but are highly suppressed by a social 'tantalization' or marital clash.

## Notes and References

1. Breakthrough in Psychotherapy For All Emotional Problems and Psychosomatic Disorders. Moudston: Londinium Press, 1979, 22.

2. M. Rajeshwar, *Indian Women Novelists and Psychoanalysis* (Atlantic, 1998), 9.

3. Kamala Markandaya "Replies to the Questionnaire," *Kakatiya Journal of English Studies*, 3 (1978): 83.

4. Mrs. Mary Wood-Allen, *What A Young Woman Ought to Know*, (London: The Vir Publishing Company), 110.

5. M. Rajeshwar, "The Unconscious Desire and its Fulfilment: Kamala Markandaya's *A Silence of Desire,*" *Indian Women Novelists and Psychoanalysis* (New Delhi: Atlantic Publishers and Distributors, 1998), 47.

6. M. Rajeshwar, "The Unconscious Desire and its Fulfilment: Kamala Markandaya's A Silence of Desire," *Indian Women Novelists and Psychoanalysis*, (New Delhi: Atlantic Publishers and Distributors, 1998), 49.

7. Elena J. Kalinnikova, *Indian English: A Survey,* 163.

8. "The Coffer Dams: A Critical Study." *Perspective on Kamala Markandaya* ed. Madhusudan Prasad, 173.

9. Yeats, "A Prayer For My Daughter," *Selected Poetry*, Pan Books, 101.

# Woman through Narrative Techniques

## 6

Kamala Markandaya's statement, 'I do write and rewrite and polish endlessly.... I cannot tell you how I know, when to stop, having achieved the effect I wanted. I simply know that that is just right; and then I stop being haunted'[1] clearly exhibits her concern for the techniques of her narrative, which she chisels, polishes and re-polishes until she gets the desired effect. She is interested in both, the 'what' and 'how' of narrative.[2] Her effective and forceful narrative techniques that include First Person Technique, Third Person Omniscient Technique, Stream of Consciousness, Interior Monologues and others project woman's renovation from possession to person while interacting with tradition and modernity. It is the magic of her narrative techniques that she draws the undivided attention of the readers who are ever inquisitive to know about what is to happen.

Kamala Markandaya makes her fictional world certainly sociological in nature by exhibiting her awareness for emerging Indian ethos particularly of the village. S.Z.H. Abidi writes, "In order to convey her sociological awareness she uses the methods and techniques of social realism."[3] The very first novel *Nectar in a Sieve* exhibits Kamala Markandaya's skill in using First Person Narrative Technique. The narrator is Rukmani, the protagonist who being a woman reveals the feminine sensibility. The great advantage of this technique is that the reader associates himself with the character and to some extent is intimate with the character. This technique also provides an outlet to the novelist to reveal his or her viewpoint. Though

Kamala Markandaya is objective and impartial to a great extent, yet she also associates herself with the protagonist who becomes her mouthpiece. She is the best when she presents Rukmani's determination and will to fight against the odds. It seems that she is expressing her own struggle in England where in the beginning she faced odd circumstances and had to do various jobs in order to earn her livelihood. The novel is set in the rural background and Rukmani narrates the story with the rural touches. The story is of rural India by a woman novelist, living in England. But, somewhere, there is the western touch that enters her language without her knowledge. The native narration is missing as it lacks Indian vigour. In spite of this, the novel *Nectar in a Sieve* is a story of a rural simple Indian woman who is optimistic, cares for her family and fights against inexorable nature, changing times, and chill poverty.

The First Person Narration is more forceful in *Some Inner Fury* than *Nectar in a Sieve*. The narrator is Mira who is from the westernized upper class society of the pre-Independence era. The technique is employed with much artistic success as it is not the story of a villager but of an emotional young woman and Kamala Markandaya is quite at ease in telling her story. The novelist narrates the story for the narrator Mira. *Some Inner Fury* is the semi-autobiographical novel. The heroine Mira is the projection of her own personality. Kamala Markandaya has shown Mira rejecting her lover for the sake of her country. In real life, she did the opposite by leaving her country for the sake of a Britisher, Taylor whom she married. Mira differs from Rukmani in her approach to life. Mira believes in the present and is not conscious of the past while Rukmani never forgets the past and is lost in gentle reminiscence.

Kamala Markandaya's deep interest lies in depicting contemporary Indian reality. She peeps into the soul of her women through the window of her heart but never steps down, as her primary concern is to narrate the story and offer the social comment though occasionally, she makes them lost in their consciousness resulting in interior monologue. She has employed quite successfully the non-omniscient third person narrative technique in *Possession* where the narrator is not the chief protagonist but Anasuya, a minor character who reports objectively. *A Silence of Desire, A Handful of Rice, The Coffer Dams, Two Virgins, The Nowhere Man, The Golden Honeycomb* and *The Pleasure City* are the stances of her Omniscient Third Person narration. *The Golden Honeycomb* presents her skill in chronological narration.

Kamala Markandaya takes the wheat of story, puts it into the machine of social set-up to get the flour of conflict. The conflict in the mind of her characters particularly women results in the dramatic element in her novel. It provides an outlet to the characters for the flowing of their inner feelings. Their person or identity comes to the fore through dialogues and conflicts in their mind. The male characters that speak of female ones show their attitude of possessiveness over them while it is the woman who unfurls a woman—the inner woman through her narration.

Rukmani, the protagonist of *Nectar in a Sieve* has an emotional attachment with the home built by her husband Nathan and is shocked when the landlord takes it.

> This home my husband had built for me with his own hands in the time he was waiting for me; brought me to it with a pride which I, used to better living, had so very nearly crushed. In it we had lain together, and our children had been born. This hut with all its memories was to be taken from us, for it stood on land that belonged to another. And the land itself by which we lived. It is a cruel thing. I thought. They do not know what they do to us. (*Nectar in a Sieve* 137)

It is with the Indian woman that she considers the home of her husband as sweet home where she gives birth to children and makes it a heavenly place for better living. Rukmani gets the hut as an unforgettable gift from her husband Nathan. She passes her time here with her children. When it is taken away, she feels uprooted and lifeless. Her narration clearly shows her concern for the home and the family. It may be simply an action of taking back the land where it stood for the landlord but for her, it is just like to take her life-breath. She has the courage to call the action of the landlord as a cruel thing. Somewhere in her, she has a latent power to fight against injustice and adverse circumstances of life.

This ongoing narration demonstrates Rukmani as a god-fearing Indian woman who has a faith in the mercy of the gods. "My mother, whenever I paid her a visit, would make me accompany her to a temple, and together we would pray and pray before the deity, imploring for help until we were giddy" (*Nectar in a Sieve* 22). An Indian woman is an image of patience, so is Rukmani who believes in gods even when her prayers are not granted. Rather she patiently defends her stance of her belief saying, "But the Gods have other things to do: they cannot attend to the pleas of every suppliant who dares to raise his cares to heaven" (*Nectar in a Sieve* 22).

From the viewpoint of an Indian man, bearing children is considered to be the most pious action on the part of an Indian woman. Nathan does not blame his son-in-law who deserts Ira because of not bearing any child. He defends him saying, "I do not blame him," Nathan said, "He is justified, for a man needs children. He has been patient." Nathan's viewpoint is the upshot of this male-oriented society. Rukmani is positive and optimistic in her approach and praises her husband saying, 'Not patient like you beloved' (54). Her husband waited for a long time for children and never thought of second marriage. Rukmani's narration proves her superiority over her husband Nathan and her reply proves her inner beauty in appreciating her husband's patience.

Nathan scolds his daughter Ira and asks her not to parade at night like a common strumpet. He wishes to show his dominance over her but it is Ira who without any hesitation, retorts, "Tonight and tomorrow and every night, so long as there is need. I will not hunger anymore" (*Nectar in a Sieve* 103) Kamala Markandaya infuses a strong determination in Ira who cares more for saving the life of her brother from death and hunger than the condemnation of the society.

In *Some Inner Fury*, Kamala Markandaya has fully exploited the First Person technique to reveal the mental struggle of Mira who sacrifices her love for the sake of her country.

> ...it was simply the time for parting. We had known love together; whatever happened the sweetness of that knowledge would always remain. We had drunk deeply of the chalice of happiness, which is not given to many even to hold. Now it was time to set it down and go (*Some Inner Fury* 285). An interior monologue is taking place in her mind when she is on the point of taking decision. Her mental horizon flashes before the readers. "Go? Leave the man I loved to go with these people? What did they mean to me, what could they mean, more than the man I loved? They were my people those other were his" (*Some Inner Fury* 285).

In this male oriented society, a man expects from a woman to cook and to bear children for him. He makes a woman parasite though he himself is parasite. It is woman who turns his house into a sweet home. In *A Handful of Rice*, Ravi thinks of a woman not as a person but as a possession. The following narration throws light on his narrow attitude and clearly reveals the fact of possessing the person:

> If I had a wife, he thought as he ate, she would cook for me, it would be like this everyday...but what had he to offer to get himself a wife.... I'll buy her a little house, small but nice... (*A Handful of Rice* 11).

It is woman who makes man forget of his trouble. Ravi thinks of Nalini: "Take a girl like that, and half a man's troubles would be over" (*A Handful of Rice* 25). He further reflects: "this girl with the bright eyes and thick, glossy hair, who could transform a man's life" (25). This notion very truly reveals the mentality of the male character that expects his transformation from her without her transformation. But it is the victory of Kamala Markandaya that she plugs such energy in her women that they have the courage to change the properties of the sea of life without any stir.

In *A Silence of Desire*, the husband Dandekar expects complete faith from his wife Saroja and when he doubts her, he loses control over himself and uses abusive terms for her. When the thread of understanding and faith becomes weak, he calls his wife a soiled woman and uses harsh language:

> Yes. And if I had watched you sooner, it would have been better for us, all of us, because a soiled woman is no good to anyone, not even to her children, do you understand that? (*A Silence of Desire* 71). His speech shows his possessiveness over his wife. But Kamala Markandaya has made Sarojini audacious enough to reply in the same coin. "You listened to the office gossip and you spied on me.... But you have eyes. If you wish to see you can. See for yourself there is nothing to stop you" (*A Silence of Desire* 73)

The woman arises in Sarojini when she finds that her husband doubts her. The above words clearly show her anger and protest against her husband. She also commits a mistake in taking her husband into confidence.

Possession changes into person. Her identity is at stake. She retorts and ultimately succeeds in making her husband realize of her person. This is the magic of Kamala Markandaya's narrative technique. It is the 'person' that makes Sarojini speak: "Sick—your brain must have been sick, to have believed what you did—to have followed me as if I were common harlot with whom you consorted but were not sure of" (*A Silence of Desire* 86-87).

Kamala Markandaya's skill lies in creating a vivid picture before the readers who are ever keen to know. Her narration makes them mesmerized. In *Two Virgins*, through her narrative technique, Kamala Markandaya depicts a picture when Devraj, the assistant of Mr. Gupta tempts Saroja to woo. "He came close. He touched her. Please, he said. Saroja leapt up. Her flesh was molten. She knew what he was asking. She knew where it ended. She had dragged her bloated gravid sister out of the bog, she had seen the bloody pulp of the baby" (*Two Virgins* 245).

Saroja's person comes to the fore and kicks the temptation of Devraj saying: "Take your hand off me." She screams, "What do you take me for 'a virgin in your whorehouse'" (*Two Virgins* 245). 'Person' dominates 'possession'. She is not a toy to be played in the hands of man. She makes Devraj realize of her own person or identity.

In *The Golden Honeycomb*, dialogues between Bawajiraj III and Mohini open up a choice either for slavery—a stage of losing identity or freedom—a stage of getting identity.

"I beg you. Will you not marry me?"

"No"

"It would make me the happiest man alive."

"I can make you happy without that. I have no wish to be your second wife either." (*The Golden Honeycomb* 32)

Bawajiraj tempts Mohini and asks her to make him the happiest man by marrying him but Mohini who could become the queen, turns down his request "I do not want to be your queen. I want to be free" (*The Golden Honeycomb* 32).

For her, her son Rabi has more importance than to be queen. She does not wish to lose her right of bringing up her son Rabi and is ready to be called as concubine. For an Indian woman, her children are her life. The above reply of Mohini clearly throws light on her identity as an Indian woman who votes for freedom against slavery.

'What a woman thinks of a woman and what a man thinks of a woman' are the two aspects of one single issue that determines the role of a woman either as a person or possession in the society. Since the society is male- dominated, the needle of the scale is forced to bend in favour of man. Now it depends on woman how she wishes to be treated. If she determines to be a person, she will be treated as such. Kamala Markandaya has awakened her female protagonists who make men realize of their importance as person. Rukmani, Mira, Sarojini, Nalini, Saroja, Mohini and Usha etc.,—all of them make their male counterparts feel that they are not inferior in any way. While following the moral code of conduct, they make men realize that they are not mere possession, but are persons. The novelist Kamala Markandaya succeeds in raising their voice through her narrative techniques. Though sometimes, in the First Person Narrative technique, she does not retain her detachment and in narrating the viewpoint of her female protagonists, it seems that the narrator is not narrating but she is doing it for the narrator. Praising Kamala Markandaya's narrative genius, S.Z.H. Abidi writes, "She manages to put across her themes and points of view in functional narratives.... Suitable manipulation of view through a variety of narrative techniques breathless narration, vivid description, objective reportage and dramatic dialogues—all join hands to make her a skilful narrative genius."[4]

## Notes and References

1. Markandaya in a letter to Margaret Joseph dated 9 Oct. 1976 quoted by Joseph in Kamala Markandaya (New Delhi: Arnold-Heinemann, 1980), 216.

2. Sunaina Kumar, *Indian Women Novelists* Set II, Vol. II, edited by R.K. Dhawan, Prestige Books, p. 54.

3. S.Z.H. Abidi, *Perspective on Kamala Markandaya*, edited by Madhusudan Prasad, 241.

4. *Ibid.*

# An Overview

## 7

A discreet study of Kamala Markandaya's works reveals that the women reflect a sense of isolation, fear, bewilderment and emotional vulnerability as a symbol not only of growth, life and fertility but also of withdrawal, regression, decay and death. It is true that in them one witnesses the typical feminist traits—sudden awakening, acute introspection, a stasis in time and action, an unthought—of ending with a definite decision. Kamala Markandaya's experiences and consciousness unfold an inner exhilaration suggesting the prelude of a fresh awakening. Her literary creations are replete with the male-female confrontation, problems of adolescence, explicit and latent pleadings for equality, liberty and self-preservation, even risking the normal safeguarding of man and conventional production of hallowed tradition.

As a woman writer, Kamala Markandaya uses her text as part of a continuing process involving her own self-definition and her emphatic identification with her character. She has feminized the world of her novels following the theory of via media. Dr. Rakhi writes: "In her writings, Kamala Markandaya shows signs of profound influence of a feminist school of writing. In her attitude to women, she is a conservative feminist, to a certain extent and feminism is implicit in her novels are a presentation of the basic fact of awakening feminine consciousness."[1]

Kamala Markandaya shows her keen interest in the relationship of the individual and society and then searches the possibilities and mechanisms of change in the individual resulting in society at large. Her investigation and presentation of feminine consciousness are directed towards an objective account of woman's emotions assessing Indian womanhood's confrontation with male reality. On making a deep perusal of her novels, one sees her intense awareness of her identity as a woman and her attention to feminine problems. She is not a radical feminist and her novels are not an outright condemnation of a repressive male-dominated society calling for radical reconstructing of male-female roles. Nor are they naturalistic accounts about the victimization of women. In the words of P. Geetha,

> Kamala Markandaya's attitude to feminism is established personal, analytic and exploratory rather than public, political or polemical.... She does not create a woman's world; but she presents the real world, sometimes raising serious question about contemporary attitude to men, women and marriage. She investigates the actual social and emotional bonds that shackle women. Indian woman in her novels defines herself by a set of relationships and modes of conduct within a created society. She confronts a tradition—oriented society and learns to live under the twin whips of heritage and modernity."[2]

Her novels are not a propaganda for reforms but they reflect the ambivalence of change in women. Being a conservative feminist, her feminism is implied in her novels.

In *Nectar in a Sieve*, Rukmani who seems to be the legendary archetype of an ideal housewife rises against the social forces confronting her retaining the sanctity of her home. In her assertions against the social forces, she emerges as a positive mature leader. While playing the traditional role, she faces the modern predicament. Home is a temple in which the mother-priestess celebrates a communion uniting the members of the family circle by means of a mystical life force. Rukmani helps in binding the family when it is shaken by the industrial revolution. She is bold enough to go to meet Dr. Kenny for medical treatment without caring the comments of this conservative society.

In *A Handful of Rice*, Nalini becomes sheet anchor of the wavering life of Ravi at the time when he, with his own masculine values, undermines the family life. Ravi feels the restoring power of Nalini in his weak moments of allurements towards Damodar's amoral world. He feels incomplete without Nalini. He cannot move a step without her guidance. He feels peace, easy and safe under her eye and care. While living according to the traditional norms, she guides her husband and instills courage in him in the critical hours of his life. Jayamma, mother of Nalini is a woman of dominating nature. She demonstrates her dominance over the family members particularly her husband. She parades it to undermine Ravi and to some extent, in the very beginning, becomes successful but, ultimately, is undermined before his masculinity.

In *A Silence of Desire*, Kamala Markandaya presents Sarojini who fights against male oriented society but she never forgets her role as wife and mother and tries her best to maintain it. Her husband Dandekar keeps his eyes closed to her feelings or problems. He is such type of husband as builds up his family life on the weak foundation of physical love. Definitely, this edifice will fall down. He does not realize this fact that a woman is more than a mother, wife or housekeeper. He neglects the fact that she has a soul. Sarojini, who is suffering from a serious ailment, does not tell him about it. Without taking her husband into confidence, she goes to the faith healer. When he comes to know about it, she still continues to go quite against his will. Finally, she gives her consent to get scientific treatment but she does so on the instruction from the Swamy. Thus, she has shown herself independent figure confronting male reality.

In *Some Inner Fury*, Kamala Markandaya introduces Premala as the representative of her feminist view of life. She is brought up in the conventional Hindu tradition and is married to the westernized Kit. What she searches in life is quite different from what he wants her to be. Meena Shirwadkar observes: "The Indian husband, even when educated, does not treat his wife as a companion but as a subordinate. However, he expects her to behave like a modern wife."[3] This double attitude and his hatred for the Indian way of life turn him into a bully and a sadist. Premala tries her best to adjust herself with her husband but fails. Her tragedy is brought about not by timidity but by the very traditional sense of duty and devotion. Once she fails as a traditional wife, she decides to go her way "tacitly acknowledging thus the imperfect articulation of their marriage" (*Some Inner Fury* 223). She takes up an orphan to occupy herself even though Kit dislikes this and the village "was becoming her world for she could find no place in the one her husband inhabited" (*Some Inner Fury* 157). She puts up a heroic struggle between her instinctual, individual urge and demands of the group. This is the victory that leads the Indian woman towards liberation.

In *Nowhere Man*, Mrs. Pickering is the lady who manifests her courage enough to face and fight the society. Though a foreigner, she is the befitting lady who can be included in the feminist group of Kamala Markandaya's characters. She is independent in thinking and attitude. She does what she likes to do. That is why she sympathizes with Srinivas who has become a nervous wreck after the loss of his beloved wife Vasantha. Both of them rise above these racial barriers and come together though in 'sinful marriage.' She supports him and stands by him in his trials and instills courage in him in the hour of his mental break down. She cares neither the quizzical look of the neighbourhood nor the curiosity of Laxman. It is her greatness that she does not leave him even when he makes the fatal announcement that he has contracted leprosy. Rather she cares him and is moved by his pitiable condition. She lives life according to her own manners clipping the strands of the social forces, which try to enmesh her completely.

In *The Coffer Dams*, it is Helen who fares better in feminist context. Neglecting her, her husband Clinton makes himself busy with his work of building the dam. She feels emotionally isolated and being frustrated, she needs an outlet, which is provided by Bashiam and the tribes. She forgets herself while exploring primitive India. Torn as she is between her instinctual and individual needs and the demands of her partner, she establishes unisexual values but at the expense of personal fulfilment and happiness. Harmony between the conservative Clinton and non-conformist wife Helen is broken.

Corinna in *Pleasure City* is another lady who is independent in her thinking and attitude. The difference is that Helen's husband tries to assert his power over her but Corinna's husband Tully never does so. Corinna comes and stays with him for a short while and packs off when the alien desert of her husband's professional site wearies her. Quite contrary to Corinna, Tully's grandmother lived with her husband just out of a sense of duty because she believed that one's place is by the husband's side. Tully wonders: "What did a man feel like, tied to a dutiful woman?" (*Pleasure City* 134). Tully respects the self in Corinna and her identity. He does not mind his wife's going away. Still, she does not seem to be happy. Western women like Helen Clinton (*The Coffer Dams*) and Mrs. Tully (*Pleasure City*) who experience a kind of dissonance in married life end up as frustrated souls. But, the Indian women in her novels get involved in wrecks; however "they come out safe, if not whole"[4] probably because the new awakening is strengthened by their traditional values as well. A remarkable thing in Kamala Markandaya's novels is her concept that success in marriage depends on mutual love and care, not on women's failure at autonomy.

Characters like Roshan, Usha, Mohini, Mira, Ira, Lalitha, Saroja etc., who are modern and progressive in their approach towards womanhood elucidate Kamala Markandaya's feminism best. Young women like Roshan and Usha are confident of their own decision power and stand firm on their feet. Mira, who runs after her romantic desires, ultimately defies the parental authority as she herself admits, "I do not remember having crossed her (mother) before" (*Some Inner Fury* 61). She breaks all bounds of convention and even takes up a journalistic career. Later, she is engulfed in the fervid flames of patriotism and very courageously sacrifices Richard for 'her people.' At this time, she is a complete woman traditional and emancipated enough to proclaim her values and priorities in life fearlessly:

I began to perceive, beneath surfaces glazed by familiarity colours and values that had not been apparent before. Moreover, the power handed to me so lightly of being able to cast my own moulds, of finding my own expressions for feelings which had hardly been evoked till now, was one which not having exercised before, I found exhilarating. (*Some Inner Fury* 94)

Usha in *The Golden Honeycomb* ties peasant garment ungracefully and shows her stamina for struggle against the British rule. She wishes to show that woman, who manages her home well, can lead in the struggle. Even in her childhood, with her revolutionary dramatic performance, she shows seeds of her leading role, which she has to play in the struggle against imperial power. The cherished dream of woman is to be someone's wife. But Mohini in *The Golden Honeycomb* is an exception. She refuses to be the legal wife, as she does not want to be tied down by such bonds as are controlled by the foreign imperial touch. Maharaja himself is governed by her—by "the narrow will of a woman, confined to women's quarters. Bounded by a woman's narrow horizon" (*The Golden Honeycomb* 71).

Ira (*Nectar in a Sieve*) becomes a prostitute under the adverse circumstances but she is not ashamed of it as she thinks it quite moral on the ground of saving her brother. Her father Nathan prevents her from moving on this path but she defies. She shows her determination and courage when she makes up her mind to bring forth the Albino child that she conceives outside wedlock. She lives by herself and shows her own wish to choose her own life.

*Two Virgins*, a feminist novel to the core, presents the view of life of a sexual, moral and cultural deviator Lalitha who fits into the definition of the liberated heroine. Diana Trilling notes in her article 'The Liberated Heroine':

She (the liberated heroine) is a fictional creation whose first concern is the exploration and realization of female self-hood, the investigation of self undertakes to the independent of the traditional dictates of society as these pertain to female behaviour and the relation of sex.[5]

Lalitha draws a colam pattern to welcome Mr. Gupta. But Gupta unconsciously reflects the hard fate she is going to suffer at his hands "When Mr. Gupta shuffled his feet the dove got blurred." (*Two Virgins* 71). She goes to the city in pursuit of stardom and becomes a victim of sex. With all the reproaches of society, she cannot face going back to the village. Even though her parents try to get the abortion done in secret, the whole course of her life changes; she chooses her own society because "she had catapulted herself outside the orbit of her community" (*Two Virgins* 163). In the image of the colam, Lalitha repairs the damage done to the pattern of dove and it turns out to be eagle and this eagle represents the worst turn the stream of her life takes.

Kamala Markandaya blesses Saroja with all the graces and tenderness of a woman's heart. The case of her sister teaches her to respect the sacredness of virginity. She represses her natural desires under the impact of the codes of the traditional society. Aunt Alamelu always reminds her of this code. She realizes that all men are responsible for their moral lives, no matter what extenuating circumstances exist. From their insight, she immediately moves to the recognition of her own responsibility. She rejects the offers of Devraj and Chingleput. There is too much to learn from the contrasting figures of the two sisters. Analysing feminism in Kamala Markandaya's novels, P. Geetha writes:

> There is a new awareness of fulfilment of feminine identities on a social and emotional and spiritual context as represented by characters like Usha, Mohini, Mira, Roshan, Saroja and Lalitha. There is a reassessment of what the woman in the Indian context aspires to. At the same time, Kamala Markandaya does not want her characters to part with the past and their ancient heritage. That amounts to a fundamental dualism in her novels—she tries to criticise the tradition which she has inherited; but at the same time in a sense tries to renew it.[6]

Indian women novelists have made their mark in Indian fiction in English. They have created novels rich in variety, thought and technique. Though primarily writing on "women subject" they have developed a style of their own. Each one of them is different from other, has her own world of experience, her own way of looking at things and her own way of portraying the characters. What one possesses, other lacks. But, Kamala Markandaya is a committed novelist who has established a tradition and prepared a path for the other women novelists.

Kamala Markandaya differs from R.P. Jhabvala in personal life as well as in professional skill. Kamala Markandaya married an Englishman and settled with him in London while R.P. Jhabvala married an Indian architect and settled down in Delhi. Both of them have affinities with each other regarding the national movement as they were affected by the partition that uprooted millions from their homesteads. R.P. Jhabvala concentrates upon family life, social problems and personal relationships with the typical Indian institution of the extended family, with all its opportunities for intrigue, clash between generations and marital feuding. She was awarded the prestigious Booker prize for *Heat and Dust* (1975), which is about two English women and their life in India 25 years before and after Independence, especially the social attitude to inter-racial sex relation. Kamala Markandaya pays equal attention to both character and environment. For R.P. Jhabvala, the social background is rather more important than the characters. She is preoccupied with the environment only with India as its focal point. In her world, human beings generally appear ludicrous.

Unlike Anita Desai, Kamala Markandaya writes with a social purpose in mind. She is more comfortable in depicting the outer world of her women than the inner one. Contrary to her, Anita Desai lives in the inner world and feels quite allergic to the outer world. She steps into the territory of the world of consciousness and fathoms the depths of the mind of her protagonists. Her women's problems are not social or economical like Kamala Markandaya but are psychological, existential and spiritual. Her forte is the exploration of sensibility and her writings reveal inner realities and psychic reverberation of her characters. Maya in *Cry, the Peacock* describes herself as 'body without a heart, heart without body.' Monisha in *Voices in the City* develops an incurable claustrophobia and commits suicide. Sita, in *Where Shall We Go This Summer?*, realizes that her marriage and all human relationships are just a farce. She is disgusted with the tedium and drabness of a meaningless life. Nanda Kaul in *Fire on the Mountain* lives like a recluse and prizes her privacy more than anything else. Her women are irritated by the sheltered over protected life reserved for them and the condescending discriminative attitude adopted towards them not only by the society but also by the family. Her novels are pleadings for the legitimate rights and freedom of such unfortunate women. Kamala Markandaya's women are not so philosophical as Anita Desai's. But they are more realistic, courageous and enthusiastic than those of Anita Desai. They struggle well and know how to live in the society.

Shashi Deshpande deals with the middle class Indian woman who represents the overwhelming majority of Indian women and is struggling to adjust in it rather than get free from the traditional world. It is on the point of adjustment that both Kamala Markandaya and Shashi Deshpande shake hands with each other. While remaining well with the bounds of the Indian society, both of them have raised some significant questions pertaining to the position of women in society and gender issues. Shashi Deshpande's female protagonists are sensitive, self-conscious, brilliant and creative. Both Jaya (*That Long Silence*) and Sarita (*The Dark Holds No Terrors*) evince the novelist's concern for women who are being misunderstood and passing through a great turmoil and suffering. There is in her novels revulsion to normal physical functions such as menstruation, pregnancy and procreation. Women, she feels, must not be reduced to the level of a breeding machine. But in the world of Kamala Markandaya, these are natural processes and there is not a single novel, which does not deal with physical functions.

Woman cannot be caged in one particular image, as she possesses myriad images in multi-coloured dimensions. While judging her, one should keep in mind that images may be different but heart cannot be changed for a woman is a woman and will remain the same. To comprehend her enigmatic personality and varied moods is to master the vagaries of nature. Yet, she is capable of performing various roles according to the seasons and necessities. She can be a loving mother, a devoted wife, a dear sister, an affectionate daughter, or a sincere mistress provided she is honoured and understood by 'the man.'

In her paper "On Images"[7] presented at a seminar on socio-literature held at the East-West Centre for Cultural Interchange in Honolulu, Hawaü, on Aug. 1, 1973, Kamala Markandaya discussed some of the ideas found in her novels. She argued that human beings have certain pre-conceptions about people, which find expression in certain images that influence behaviour with others. This attitude of an individual to another individual broadens into the attitude of a nation to another nation. With a crusader's zeal, she is out for the "demolitions of images"[8] and for the "rejection of fantasy in favour of truth."[9] She abhors discrimination, exploitation or any type of cruelty against women. She writes: "I do detest racism in any form just as I detest cruelty to any living being."[10]

Though basically, Kamala Markandaya has projected the traditional image of woman, it will be injustice to carve her woman in this image as she has rediscovered, redefined and asserted her identity as person, not as possession. Feeling the pulse of the changed time, she has created a new race of woman who is neither staunch traditionalist nor ultra-modern but that who honours the traditions and welcomes modernity to the best of her calibre and sensibility. She can very intelligently keep pace with the new developments of the fast electronic world. To create such new race, she has taken up the most vitalizing stuff of tradition along with the purest light stuff of modernity. This light stuff of modernity has now entered her soul electrifying the moral strength, which expresses itself at the surface in the form of her equipoise.

By creating the new image of woman, Kamala Markandaya has emerged as a bridge builder between the tradition and modernity. It seems that she agrees with Mrs. Mary Wood-Allen who inspires young girls making them more and more to feel:

> A sacred burden is this life ye bear.
> Look on it, lift it, bear it solemnly.
> Stand up and walk beneath it steadfastly.
> Fail not for sorrow, falter not for sin,
> But onward, upward, till the goal ye win."[11]

Kamala Markandaya's women like Rukmani who is conscious of her self-esteem and duties to the family, sees various possibilities of life; Ira who wins the hearts of the readers with her heroic self-sacrifice, slaps the face of the so-called society by showing her courage in bringing up the sickly albino; Mira who values love over marriage and favours the marriage of two minds, forsakes her lover Richard for her country; Roshan who symbolizes the resurgence of Indian women in the wake of the national movement, is truly Indian at heart; Premala who sets an example by her preference to serve the group, is traditional; Sarojini who suffers a lot due to her silence, finds her way in faith and understanding to save the family; Caroline whose jealousy for Annabel and Ellie makes her feminine, is a model of anti-patriarchal stance; Anasuya who is well aware of Indian tradition and culture; proves to be a frail bridge between eastern and western world, Nalini who with her sanity and realism takes out her husband from the mud of amoral world; Helen who longs for Indian spiritualism, believes in religion of humanity based on love and fellow-feelings; Mrs. Pickerings who cares for Srinivas, is the most balanced woman with her mature attitude; Vasantha who is truly Indian remains a devoted wife throughout her life; Lalitha who repents and takes the fork to commit suicide, is a virgin in a whorehouse; Saroja who is quite satisfied with the life of her village, is not misled by the attractions for the modern world like her sister; Manjula who expresses her grievance, persuades Mohini not to marry Bawajiraj III; Mohini who longs for freedom of thought, hates to be queen at the cost of her freedom; Usha who inspires the fighters for freedom, makes plan with Rabi for future; Valli who takes up her share of the household tasks gives a good performance as a sales assistant in the Shalimar Gift Shop and Emporium; Corinna who in spite of being a great admirer of art, wishes to live in her own world; Mrs. Contractor who with her practical approach, manages all the activities of Shalimar; Mrs. Lovat who is devoted to her profession of writing, believes that women are not inferior to men—are exemplary and acquaint the readers with Indian culture and values.

This new image has given a ray of hope and a goal to the countless women who are groping in the dark and living in isolation and frustration. Kamala Markandaya has opened a new vista for women by infusing a crusading spirit into them for the welfare of humanity and the alleviation of human suffering.

Kamala Markandaya has presented the Indian food in the western plate. While doing so, sometimes she crosses the limit and forgets the ethos of Indian culture in order to please the western readers for whom she was writing. Like Shakespeare who introduced the supernatural element, she paints the pages of her novels with the red colour—sex, naked picture, virginity, and first night after marriage etc. But it is she who initiated the lead of women's transformation from possession to person through her novels. She has succeeded in reviving the values and traditions, which were moribund. Her novels are universal in appeal and have a place of pride in their own right in the field of Indian English Fiction. It is not accidental that her works have been translated into many languages. This recognition has been brought to her by her works, which portray women and the basic reality of Indian society in a sensitive and authentic manner. She represents the great tradition of women novelists established by Jane Austen. She has broken the monopoly of the Big three—Raja Rao, Mulk Raj Anand and R.K. Narayan and secured a permanent place in the firmament of Indian English fiction.

## Notes and References

1. "Kamala Markandaya's *Nectar in a Sieve*: As a Feminist Poetics," *Indian Writing in English* Vol. III ed. 108.

2. Feminism in The Novels of Kamala Markandaya" *Indian Women Novelists,* Set II, Vol. II, ed. by R.K. Dhawan, (New Delhi: Prestige) 10.

3. *Image of Woman in The Indo-Anglian Novel,* (New Delhi: Sterling, 1979), 57.

4. P.S. Chauhan, "Kamala Markandaya, Sense and Sensibility," *The Literary Criterion,* XII (2 & 3): 146.

5. Diana Trilling, "The Liberated Heroine" *Partisan Review,* 4 (1978): 501.

6. P. Geetha, "Feminism in The Novels of Markandaya," *Indian Women Novelists* Set II, ed. R.K. Dhawan (New Delhi: Prestige) 21.

7. *Ibid.,* 9. (Quoted from the Xerox copy of the paper sent to the writer of this Article by Mrs. Margaret Joseph who got a copy of the original paper from Prof. Dorothy B. Shimmer, formerly of the Department of English in Honolulu University, Hawaü).

8. *Ibid.,* 12

9. *Ibid.*

10. Quoted Margaret P. Joseph, *Kamala Markandaya,* 214.

11. Mrs. Mary Wood-Allen, *What A Young Woman Ought to Know* (London: The Vir Publishing Company), 17.

# Selected Bibliography

## A. Novels by Kamala Markandaya

*Nectar in a Sieve*, New York: Signet Books, 1954.

*Some Inner Fury*, London: Putnam & Co., 1955.

*A Silence of Desire*, London: Putnam & Co., 1960.

*Possession*, London: Putnam & Co., 1963.

*A Handful of Rice*, New Delhi: Orient Paperbacks, 1966.

*The Coffer Dams*, Delhi: Hind Pocket Books, 1969.

*The Nowhere Man* (Originally published in 1972), reprinted, Bombay: Orient Longman (Sangam Books), 1975.

*Two Virgins* (Originally published in 1973), reprinted, Vikas Publishing House, 1975.

*The Golden Honeycomb*, New Delhi: B.I. Publication, 1977.

*Pleasure City*, London: Chatto & Windus, 1982.

## B. Books on Kamala Markandaya

Joseph, Margaret P. *Kamala Markandaya*. New Delhi: Arnold Heinemann (Indian Writers Series—17), 1980.

Prasad, Madhusudan. *Perspectives on Kamala Markandaya*. Ghaziabad: Vimal Prakashan (Indo-English Writers Series—5)

Bhatnagar Anil Kumar. *Kamala Markandaya: A Thematic Study*. New Delhi: Sarup & Sons, 1995.

Bhatnagar M.K., *Kamala Markandaya: A Critical Spectrum*. New Delhi: Atlantic Publishers and Distributors.

Misra Pravati, *Class Consciousness in the Novels of Kamala Markandaya*. New Delhi: Atlantic Publishers and Distributors.

## C. Critical Articles on Kamala Markandaya in Journals

Appaswamy, S.P. "The Golden Honeycomb: A Saga of Princely India by Kamala Markandaya," *The Journal of Indian Writing in English*. Vol. 6, No. 2. July 1978.

Betty Friedman. *The Second Stage*. New York: Summit Books, 1981.

Carol Gilligan. *In a Different Voice*. Cambridge: Havard University Press, 1982.

Chandrasekharan, K.R. "East and West in the Novels of Kamala Markandaya" *Critical Essays on Indian writing in English*. M.K. Naik, et. al. (Dharwar) University of Dharwar in Collaboration with Macmillan Co. of India, 1968.

Chauhan, P.S. "Kamala Markandaya: Sense and Sensibility" *The Literary Criterion*. Vol. XII, Nos. 2-3, 1976.

Das, Bijay Kumar. "Kamala Markandaya's Novels: Critical Introduction", *The Mahanadi Review*. Vol. 1, No. 1, ed. Jagdeb, P.K.

Dubey, S.C. "Gender Relation", *Indian Society*. National Book Trust, India, 1990.

Elaine Showalter. *A Literature of Their Own, British Women Novelists From Bronte to Lessing*. Princeton, N.J.: Princeton University Press, 1977.

Ezekiel, Nissim. (Review of Kamala Markandaya's Possession), Imprint, February 1964, 188-193. "Puppet Show" (review of Kamala Markandaya's Two Virgins), *The Illustrated Weekly of India*. June 15, 1975, 32.

Geetha, P. "Kamala Markandaya—an Interpretation" *Commonwealth Quarterly*. Vol. 3, No. 9, December 1978.

Geetha, P. "Feminism in the Novels of Kamala Markandaya" *Indian Women Novelists*. Set II, Vol. II, Edited by R.K. Dhawan.

Ghosal, Madhumita and Mehru, M. Major. "The Indian Scenario in the Novels of Kamala Markandaya: An Assessment of Popular Indian Superstitions and Beliefs" *Indian Women Novelists*. Set II, Vol. II, Edited by R.K. Dhawan.

Harrex, S.C. "A Sense of Identity: The Novels of Kamala Markandaya" *Journal of Commonwealth Literature*. No. 1, June 1977.

*Indian Council of Social Science*. "Status of Women in India! A Synopsis of The National Committee on The Status of Women" (1971-74). New Delhi: Allied Publishers, 1975.

Jain, Jasbir. "The Novels of Kamala Markandaya," *Indian Literature* 18, No. 2, April-June 1975.

Jaya Baliga, "Being and Becoming: The Quest of Three Women in Some Inner Fury" *Indian Women Novelists*. Set II, Ed. by R.K. Dhawan.

Karunakar, Pria. "Village Rhythm" (Review of Kamala Markandaya's *Two Virgins*) *Youth Times*. Sept. 19, 1975, 49.

Kumar, Shiv K. "Tradition and Change in the Novels of Kamala Markandaya," *Osmania Journal of English Studies* Vol. VII, No. 1, 1969.

Lee R. Edwards. *Psyche As Hero: Female Heroism and Fictional Form*. Middle Town, Weslegan University Press, 1984.

Madhu Kishwar. "Dowry—To Ensure Her Happiness or to Disinherit Her?" *Manushi*. A Journal about Women and Society, May-June 1986.

Malvika Karlekar. "Woman's Nature and the Access to Education," ed. Karuna Chanana, *Socialization, Education and Women*. New Delhi: Orient Longman, 1988.

Mennon Madhavi. "Review of Pleasure City," *The Journal of Indian Writing in English*: 11, No. 2. (July, 1983), p. 58.

Veera Desai and Kreshnaraj Maithregi. *Women and Society in India*. New Delhi: Ajanta Publications, 1987.

Parameswaran, Uma. "India for the Western Reader: A Study of Kamala Markandaya's Novels." *Texas Quarterly* Vol. X, No. 2, Summer 1968.

Parasad, Hari Mohan. "The Quintessence of Kamala Markandaya's Art," *Commonwealth Quarterly*. Vol. 3, No. 9, December 1978.

Partha Mukherji. "Sex, Social Structure," Ed. Karuna Chanana, *Socialization, Education and Women*. New Delhi: Orient Longman, 1988.

Rachael Brownstein. *Becoming a Heroine*. New York: The Viling Press, 1982.

Rajeshwar M. *Indian Women Novelists and Psychoanalysis*. New Delhi: Atlantic Publishers and Distributors, 1998.

Rao, K.S. Narayana. "Love, Sex, Marriage and Morality in Kamala Markandaya's Novels," *The Osmania Journal of English Studies* 10 (1973).

Rao, Vimala. "Kamala Markandaya—Some First Impression," *The Literary Criterion*. Winter, 1958.

Rao, Vimala. "Indian Expatriates," *Journal of Commonwealth Literature* Vol. X, No. 3, April 1976.

Spencer Sharon. "Feminist Criticism and Literature," *American Literature Today*. Ed. Richard Kostelanentz (Forum Series, 1982), 11, 157.

Srivastava, Ramesh K. *Six Indian Novelists in English*. Guru Nanak Dev University, Amritsar, 1987.

Sudipta, B. "A Feminist Perspective of Women Characters in the Novels of Virginia Woolf and Kamala Markandaya," *Indian Women Novelists*. Set II, Vol. II, Ed. by R.K. Dhawan.

Sundaram, P.S. "The Virgins and The Prince" (review of Kamala Markandaya's *Two Virgins*," *The Hindustan Times Weekly* October 19, 1975, 10.

Susan Seifert, *The Dilemma of the Talented Heroine*. Montreal: Eden Press, 1978.

Taneja, G.R. "Deconstructing Feminism: Nectar in a Sieve—The Phenomenon of Change," *Indian Women Novelists*. Set II, Ed. by R.K. Dhawan.

Venkateswaran, Shyamala. "The Language of Kamala Markandaya's Novels," *The Literary Criterion* Vol. IX, No. 3, Winter 1970.

William Haydn. " Victims and Virgins: Some Characters in Markandaya's Novels," *Indian Women Novelists*. Set II, Vol. II, Ed. by R.K. Dhawan.

## D. General Studies of Indian-English Literature

Derrott. "The Modern Indian Novel in English: A Comparative Approach." Brussels, 1966, 152.

*Feminism and Literature* Ed. by Veena Nobel Dass. New Delhi: Prestige Books.

*Feminism and Recent Fiction in English*. Ed. by Sushila Singh. New Delhi: Prestige Books.

Galbraith, John Kenneth. *Galbraith Introduces*. India. New Delhi: Vikas, 1974.

Iyengar, K.R. Srinivasa. *Indian Writing in English*. New Delhi: Sterling Publishers Pvt. Ltd.

Kalinnikova, Elena J. *Indian English Literature: A Survey*. Ghaziabad: Vimal Prakashan, 1982.

McCutchnion, David. *Indian Writing in English*. Calcutta: Writers Workshop, 1969.

Mehta, P.P. *Indo-Anglian Fiction* (Second Revised). Bareilly: Prakash Book Depot, 1979.

Mukherjee, Meenakshi. *The Twice Born Fiction: Themes and Techniques of the Indian Novel in English*. New Delhi: Arnold Heinemann, 1971.

Naik, M.K. *Critical Essays on Indian Writing in English*. Madras: The Macmillan Company of India, 1977.

Naik, M.K. *Aspects of Indian Writing in English*. Madras: The Macmillan Company of India, 1979.

Narasimhaiah, C.D. *Fiction and The Reading Public in India*. University of Mysore, 1967.

Nicholson, Kal. *Social Problems in the Indo-Anglian and the Anglo-Indian Novel*. Bombay: Jaico, 1972.

Paramashwaran, Uma. *A Study of Representative Indo-English Novelists*. New Delhi: Vikas Publishing House, 1979.

Rao, A.V. Krishna. *The Indo-Anglian Novel and The Changing Tradition*. Mysore: Rao and Raghvan, 1972.

Sanyal, Samares C. *Indianness in Major Indo-English Novels*. Bareilly: Prakash Book Depot, 1984.

Shoma Chatterji. *The Indian Woman's Search For An Identity*. New Delhi: Vikas Publishing House, 1988.

Singh, R.S. *Indian Novels in English*. New Delhi: Arnold Heinemann, 1977.

Shirwadkar, Meena. *Image of Woman in the Indo-Anglian Novel*. New Delhi: Sterling Publisher Private Ltd., 1979.

Shantha Krshnaswamy. *The Woman in Indian Fiction in English*. New Delhi: Ashish Publishing House, 1984.

Srivastava, Sharad. *The New Woman in Indian English Fiction*. New Delhi: Creative Books.

Varma, R.M. *Some Aspects of Indo-English Fiction*. New Delhi: Jainsons, 1985.

Verghese, C. Paul. *Problems of the Indian Creative Writing in English*. Bombay: N.V. Publications, 1971.

Verghese, C. Paul. *Essays on Indian Writing in English*. Bombay: N.V. Publications, 1975.

Williams, H.M. *Indo-Anglian Literature 1800-1970 (A Survey)*. Madras: Orient Longman, 1976.

# Index

*A Handful of Rice*, 4-5, 11, 13, 21, 29, 56-59, 85-86, 106-110, 121, 123, 129

*A Silence of Desire*, 4-6, 20, 24, 26-27, 48-51, 83-84, 103, 121, 124, 129

Amma, 67-68, 71, 115

Anasuya, 5-6, 17, 28, 51-52, 71, 106, 137

Anita Desai, 1, 9, 134-35

Annabel, 20, 84-85, 105, 137

Appa, 32

Apu (*A Handful of Rice*), 13, 57, 108

Apu (*Pleasure City*), 33

Arjun, 39

Aunt Alamelu, 64, 133

Avalon, 70

Baily, 30

Bashiam, 60-61, 87, 110-11, 130

Bawajiraj II, 17, 91

Bawajiraj III, 17, 66, 91-93, 125, 138

Bill, 31

Biswas, 18

Boyle, 96

Carmen, 33

Caroline Bell, 5, 14, 17, 20, 25, 28, 51-54, 71, 85, 89, 105-06, 137

Chingleput, 15, 22, 65, 133

Clinton, 21, 30, 60, 87, 111, 130-31

Cordelia, 58

Corinna, 33, 67, 95-96, 116-17, 131, 138

*Cry, The Peacock*, 135

Damodar, 21, 29, 129

Dandekar, 20, 26-27, 49, 83, 103-05, 124, 129

Deshpande, Shashi, 1, 9, 135

Devraj, 22, 113, 124-25, 133

Dodamma, 48

Dr. Kenny, 18-19, 24, 26, 39, 42, 59, 60, 67, 101, 128

Dr. Radcliffe, 31, 89

Ellie, 20, 52, 54, 105-06, 137

Faulkner, 90

*Fire on the Mountain*, 135

First Person Technique, 119-20, 123, 126

Fred, 22, 31, 112

Govind, 16, 20, 27, 45, 81, 83, 102

Hardy, 76

*Heat and Dust*, 134

Helen, 5-6, 21, 30, 59-61, 71, 86-89, 98, 110-11, 130-31, 137

Hickey, 27, 45, 102
Hosain Attia, 1

Interior Monologue, 119
Iravady, 13, 41, 43, 76-77, 98, 122, 131-32, 137

Janaki, 39, 114
Jaya, 114
Jaya (*That Long Silence*), 135
Jayamma, 5, 13-14, 21, 58, 59, 108-10, 129
Jhabvala, R.P., 1, 9, 134
Jijabai, 18
Joe, 31
Joycean Ulysses, 8

Kali, 39
Kali (*Pleasure City*), 70
Kamala Purnaiya, 1
Kandan, the Patriot, 82
Kitchen Culture, 35
Kitsmay, 14, 16, 19-20, 27, 44-46, 79, 80, 102, 129
Kunthi, 13, 18-19, 42, 77, 101
Kuti (*Nectar in a Sieve*), 13, 39, 41-43, 76

Lalitha, 5, 15, 22, 32, 63-65, 89-91, 98, 113, 131-33, 137
Laxman, 22, 31, 62, 88

Manjula, 66, 71, 91-93, 137
Maurya, 43
Maya, 135
Mike, 31
Millie Rawlings, 30, 60
Mirabai, 5-6, 16, 20, 43-48, 60, 71, 77-78, 81, 98, 102, 120, 123, 125, 131, 133, 137

Mohini, 5, 18, 23, 66, 71, 91-93, 98, 125, 131-133, 138
Monisha, 135
Mr. Gupta, 15, 22, 32, 65, 90, 114, 124, 133
Mr. Glass, 31
Mrs. Bridie, 23, 67-68, 71, 95, 115-16
Mrs. Chari, 67
Mrs. Contractor, 15, 67, 96, 138
Mrs. Fletcher, 22, 31, 112
Mrs. Lockwood, 67
Mrs. Lovat, 67, 97, 138
Mrs. Pearl, 5, 33, 67, 69-71
Mrs. Pickering, 5, 31, 88-89, 110, 130, 137
Mulk Raj Anand, 18, 138
Murugan, 39
Muthu, 68, 94

Nalini, 5, 13-14, 21, 29, 56-59, 71, 85-86, 98, 106-09, 123, 125, 129, 137
Nanda Kaul, 135
Narayan, R.K., 138
Nathan, 12-13, 19, 24, 26, 37, 76, 116, 121-22, 132
*Nectar in a Sieve*, 4-6, 11, 18-19, 24, 26, 37-43, 59, 69, 75, 101, 116, 119-22, 128

Oliver Kim, 2

Padmani, 37
*Pleasure City*, 4-5, 7, 11, 14, 15, 23, 32, 66-70, 94-97, 115-17, 121, 131
Poor Old Granny, 13, 18-19, 39, 42
*Possession*, 4-6, 11, 14, 16-17, 20, 24-25, 28, 51-56, 84, 89, 105-06, 121

Premala, 5, 14, 16, 20, 27, 46-48, 71, 77, 79, 82, 129, 130, 137

Puttanna, 57-58, 108

Quit India Movement, 3, 16, 20, 43, 46

Rabindranath, 17-18, 23, 32, 66, 71, 92-93, 114-15, 125, 138

Raja, 39, 43

Raja Rao, 138

Rajam, 104

Rajeshwari, 82

Raju, 14, 21

Rau, Santa Ram, 1

Ravi, 13, 21, 29, 57-58, 71, 86, 106, 108-10, 123, 129

Richard, 20, 27, 43-44, 78-79, 102-03, 137

*Riders to the Sea*, 43

Rikki, 23, 32-33, 66-69, 94-97, 115-16

Roshan, 5, 77-78, 80-82, 98, 131, 133, 137

Rukmani, 5-6, 11, 13, 18-19, 24, 26-27, 37-43, 69, 71, 75-76, 98, 101, 116, 119-22, 125, 128, 137

Ruskin, 33

Sahgal, Nayantara, 1, 8-9, 73

Sarita, 135

Saroja, 5-6, 15, 22, 32, 63-65, 71, 89-91, 113, 124-25, 131, 133, 137

Sarojini, 5-6, 20, 26, 28, 49-51, 71, 83-84, 103, 105, 124-25, 129, 137

Savitri, 6, 37

Selvam, 37, 39, 43

Seshu, 62, 88

Shakespeare, 138

Shalimar Complex, 15, 32, 70, 94, 96-97, 138

Shanta, 37

Shivaji, 18

Sir Arthur, 17, 32, 66

Sita (Anita Desai), 135

Sita (*The Ramayan*), 6, 58

Socio-ecological colour, 11, 14, 26, 30, 33

Socio-economic colour, 11, 33

Socio-political colour, 11, 16, 33

Socio-psychological colour, 11, 18, 23, 33

Socio-religious colour, 11, 26, 33

*Some Inner Fury*, 4-6, 11, 14, 16, 19, 27, 37, 43-48, 60, 77-82, 102-03, 120, 123, 129-32

Sophie, 32

Srinivas, 21, 61-63, 88-89, 110-13, 130, 137

Stream of Consciousness, 119

Swamy (*A Silence of Desire*), 20, 26, 28, 51 104-05

Swamy (*Possession*), 17, 25, 105

Synge, J.M., 43

Taylor Bertrand, 2

Temple Drake, 90

Tennyson, 7

Tess of D'urbervilles, 76

Thambi, 39

Thangam, 37, 56, 58, 108

*That Long Silence*, 135

*The Coffer Dams*, 4-6, 21, 30, 59-61, 86-88, 110, 121, 130

*The Dark Holds No Terrors*, 135

*The Golden Honeycomb*, 4-6, 16-17, 23, 32, 65-66, 74, 91-93, 114, 121, 125, 132

*The Nowhere Man*, 4-5, 21-22, 31, 61-63, 88-89, 110-112, 121, 130

The Tannery, 40

Third Person Omniscient Technique, 119

Tully, 23, 32-33, 66, 94-95, 116, 131

*Two Virgins*, 4-6, 11, 15, 22, 32, 37, 63-65, 89-91, 113, 121, 124, 132-33

Usha, 5, 18, 23, 66, 74, 91-93, 98, 115, 125, 131-33, 138

Val, 14, 17, 20, 25, 28, 51-56, 89, 105-06

Valli, 23, 33, 67, 94, 98, 138

Vasantha, 5-6, 22, 31, 61-63, 71, 88-89, 111-12, 137

Venkataramani, K.S., 82

Vimla, 115

*Voices in the City*, 135

*Where Shall We Go This Summer*, 135

Wilkins, 30

Wordsworth, 2

Zevera, 67, 70